Assessment of Joint All Domain Command and Control Requirements and the Use of Live, Virtual, and Constructive Capabilities for Training

TIMOTHY MARLER, CARRA S. SIMS, MARK TOUKAN, AJAY K. KOCHHAR, SHAWN COCHRAN, CHRISTINE KISTLER LACOSTE, MATT STRAWN

Prepared for the Department of the Air Force
Approved for public release; distribution unlimited

 PROJECT AIR FORCE

For more information on this publication, visit **www.rand.org/t/RRA985-2**.

About RAND

The RAND Corporation is a research organization that develops solutions to public policy challenges to help make communities throughout the world safer and more secure, healthier and more prosperous. RAND is nonprofit, nonpartisan, and committed to the public interest. To learn more about RAND, visit www.rand.org.

Research Integrity

Our mission to help improve policy and decisionmaking through research and analysis is enabled through our core values of quality and objectivity and our unwavering commitment to the highest level of integrity and ethical behavior. To help ensure our research and analysis are rigorous, objective, and nonpartisan, we subject our research publications to a robust and exacting quality-assurance process; avoid both the appearance and reality of financial and other conflicts of interest through staff training, project screening, and a policy of mandatory disclosure; and pursue transparency in our research engagements through our commitment to the open publication of our research findings and recommendations, disclosure of the source of funding of published research, and policies to ensure intellectual independence. For more information, visit www.rand.org/about/research-integrity.

RAND's publications do not necessarily reflect the opinions of its research clients and sponsors.

Published by the RAND Corporation, Santa Monica, Calif.
© 2023 RAND Corporation
RAND® is a registered trademark.

Library of Congress Cataloging-in-Publication Data is available for this publication.
ISBN: 978-1-9774-1060-3

Cover: Shelton Keel/U.S. Air Force.

About This Report

This report presents findings addressing the potential use of live, virtual, and constructive (LVC) simulation capabilities for continuation training at Air Operation Centers in the U.S. Air Force (USAF), in support of Joint All Domain Command and Control (JADC2). The study used multiple methods, including reviews of USAF policy and other documentation, research literature, and industry trends and interviews of subject-matter experts. This report is intended for multiple audiences: the Operational Test and Training Infrastructure community in the USAF, especially those whose interest lies in the domain of modeling and simulation; the USAF community working with LVC and JADC2; and to some extent, the broader U.S. Department of Defense training community.

The research reported here was commissioned by Department of the Air Force, AF/A3T, and conducted within the Workforce, Development, and Health Program of RAND Project AIR FORCE as part of a fiscal year 2021 project, "Assessment of Joint All Domain Command and Control Requirements and the Use of Live, Virtual, and Constructive Capabilities for Training."

RAND Project AIR FORCE

RAND Project AIR FORCE (PAF), a division of the RAND Corporation, is the Department of the Air Force's (DAF's) federally funded research and development center for studies and analyses, supporting both the United States Air Force and the United States Space Force. PAF provides the DAF with independent analyses of policy alternatives affecting the development, employment, combat readiness, and support of current and future air, space, and cyber forces. Research is conducted in four programs: Strategy and Doctrine; Force Modernization and Employment; Resource Management; and Workforce, Development, and Health. The research reported here was prepared under contract FA7014-16-D-1000.

Additional information about PAF is available on our website:
www.rand.org/paf/

This report documents work originally shared with the DAF on September 24, 2021. The draft report, issued on September 30, 2021, was reviewed by formal peer reviewers and DAF subject-matter experts.

Acknowledgments

The authors thank the senior leaders at Air Force A3T. In particular, Steven Ruehl, associate deputy director of operations, and our action officer, Lillian Campbell-Wynn of AF/Air Force Agency for Modeling and Simulation (AFAMS), provided valuable oversight, guidance, and expert feedback throughout the course of our work. In addition, we thank Col Robert Epstein and

Lt Col Mark Weger, of the AFAMS, who were instrumental in initiating and guiding this study. We also thank the following USAF representatives who provided additional feedback on preliminary products: Maj Daniel Cervantes, John McDowall, Russ Mayes, Amy Stephens, Edward Degnan, Karl Kraan, Allan Fluharty, Lt Col Jason Baker, Lt Col Omar Nava, Lt Col Paul Hayes, Lt Col Tammara Alexander, and Sonia Vonderlippe.

The project team is grateful for the input from many subject-matter experts from across the USAF. In particular, we would like to thank representatives from the many organizations that provided input for our analysis: Headquarters Air Force, Joint National Training Center, Air Combat Command, Air Force Research Lab, AFAMS, the 505th Training Squadron, the 16th Air Force, Kessel Run, Shadow Operations Center-Nellis, Air Force Warfighting Integration Capability, Air Force Life Cycle Management Center, U.S. Space Force, Air Force Warfare Center, Pacific Air Force, Joint Staff (JS) J6, JS J7, Under Secretary of Defense for Research and Engineering, Naval Information Warfare Center-Pacific, U.S. Marine Corps, and U.S. Indo-Pacific Command.

At the RAND Corporation, we thank Nelson Lim, director of the Workforce, Development, and Health Program, as well as Kirsten Keller and Miriam Matthews, for their support and guidance. Julie Ann Tajiri was extremely helpful in addressing edits and references. John Ausink provided valuable insight throughout the study. Finally, we thank our reviewers, Matt Walsh and Tom Schnell, for valuable feedback and insight.

Summary

As the anticipated character of warfare changes, new operational concepts emerge in response to new needs, and training must also adapt to support these concepts and ensure readiness. Given the speed at which concepts develop and the length of time it may take to adapt training after the fact, it is prudent to assess training capabilities and practices as concepts mature rather than after concepts have been fully operationalized. Joint All Domain Command and Control (JADC2) is emerging as the preeminent operational concept. It is intended to improve situational awareness, improve abilities to direct forces across domains and services, and facilitate rapid decisionmaking. Distributed sensors, shooters, and data from all domains are connected to joint forces, enabling the coordinated exercise of authority to integrate planning and synchronize convergence in time, space, and purpose. However, JADC2 is under development by all the services as well as the Joint Staff, and therefore, plans for its execution are not yet mature. It is a complex and networked concept, and training to support this concept will require preemptive consideration of supporting capabilities, especially when considering continuation training for air operation centers. Live, virtual, and constructive (LVC) simulations can help support the complex training JADC2 will require, but proper development and deployment will require aligning training processes, LVC capabilities, and JADC2 training needs.

Approach

Project AIR FORCE leveraged extensive interviews with subject-matter experts, a systematic series of discussions with air operations center (AOC) representatives, and a review of policy, research, and development literature. JADC2-relevant training needs, processes, and capabilities were assessed for the U.S. Air Force in general and for each AOC across the air, space, and cyber domains. Capabilities and training processes were mapped back to training requirements identified early in the study. Opportunities for leveraging LVC most effectively were identified and presented as a summary of how LVC can support JADC2.

Conclusions

- JADC2 intent, capabilities, and supporting roles risk being unclear across echelons.
- Integration of multiple domains poses a cultural challenge.
- LVC-related capabilities can help support training for JADC2-related tasks at AOCs.
- Balancing centralized coordination with decentralized training needs will be critical.

  - Centralized LVC resources may be key to executing the complex needs.

- AOCs support training exercises but are less involved as a primary training audience.

- Given the operational and technical complexity of JADC2, as well as its inherently joint nature, there is a risk of siloed capability development.

Recommendations

- The JADC2 cross-functional team (CFT) should lead the distribution of a well-coordinated portfolio of material concerning JADC2 goals, plans, and capabilities.
- In collaboration with AF/A3T, the 505th Combat Training Group should leverage initial qualification training as a mechanism for centralized coordination of command and control (C2) training.
- With oversight from AF/A3T, AOCs should focus on continuation training that involves the complete AOC staff and not just individual sections or units.
- The 505th Combat Training Group and each AOC should incorporate training scenarios that test cultural norms, preparing leadership for potential changes in the delegation of authority and contested C2.
- AF/A3T should consider opportunities to leverage LVC more extensively per Table S.1, which summarizes opportunities and frameworks for illustrating how LVC may be valuable.
- All aspects of training should involve increased focus on tasking processes and capabilities *across* domains.
- The JADC2 CFT and Joint Staff J7 should leverage developing and existing distributed training systems for JADC2.
- AF/A3T should work with combatant commands, combat support agencies, other services, and major commands to enhance AOC training with space and cyber effects.

Table S.1. Opportunities to Leverage LVC for Supporting JADC2

Opportunities for Supporting JADC2	LVC Relevance
Potential changes in air tasking order (ATO) process	• This would be useful in most stages of the ATO cycle. • Reduce unnecessary white-carding[a] with ATO training. • Facilitate higher fidelity and more-complex in-house training at AOCs.
Potential changes in AOC structure	• Prepare for and enable distributed AOC structure, allowing integration of multiple C2 nodes. • Enable training for cloud-based AOC structure. • Allow integration with more-extensive simulation capabilities not available at all AOCs.
Increased use of distributed training exercises	• Enable increased accessibility and participation. • Reduce unnecessary white-carding, allowing more AOCs to garner training benefits from exercises rather than just support exercises.
Development of distributed training architectures	• Provide an integral and necessary keystone for distributed training. • Allow testing of existing and new distributed training federations and capabilities.
Development of a common information technology architecture	• Provide testing and training capabilities to include space and cyber systems. • Align the software acquisitions process for test, training, and AOC operational systems.

[a] In this context *white-carding* refers to the practice of artificially introducing an event in a simulated exercise rather than having or using the ability to actually simulate that event.

Contents

Figures

Tables

Chapter 1. Introduction

Problem and Motivation

As the anticipated character of warfare changes, new operational concepts emerge in response to new needs, and training must also adapt to support these concepts and ensure readiness. Given the speed at which concepts may develop and the length of time it may take to adapt training after the fact, it is prudent to assess training capabilities and practices as concepts mature rather than after concepts have been fully operationalized. The development and use of training capabilities must derive from and respond to the appropriate training goals and needs.[1]

In large part as a response to near-peer adversaries, warfare involves exponential growth in the amounts of data processed as well as decisionmaking at increased speeds. Consequently, Joint All Domain Command and Control (JADC2) is emerging as the preeminent operational concept to enable rapid processing and informed decisionmaking at all echelons of organizations. The Chief of Staff of the Air Force advocated for an enhanced command and control (C2) system in the congressional budget. JADC2 is defined in U.S. Air Force (USAF) doctrine as follows:

> the art and science of decision-making to rapidly translate decisions into action, leveraging capabilities across all-domains and with mission partners to achieve operational and information advantage in both competition and conflict.[2]

It is intended to improve situational awareness, improve abilities to direct forces across domains and services, and facilitate rapid decisionmaking. This concept centers on understanding the battlespace in real time to achieve mission objectives, minimize dangers posed by enemy threats, and integrate weapon systems to yield enhanced results.[3] Ideally, distributed sensors, shooters, and data from all domains are connected to joint forces, enabling the coordinated exercise of authority to integrate planning and synchronize convergence in time, space, and purpose.[4]

However, JADC2 is under development by all the services as well as the Joint Staff, and therefore, plans for its execution are not yet mature. Consequently, aligning capabilities with objectives requires careful analysis. JADC2 is a complex and networked concept, and training to

---

[1] In this context, *needs* refers to training objectives, requirements, and capabilities that airmen must be trained on but not necessarily to gaps in facilities and/or capabilities.

[2] Air Force Doctrine Note 1-20, *USAF Role in Joint All-Domain Operations*, Department of the Air Force, March 5, 2020.

[3] David Deptula and Douglas A. Birkey, "Potential Defense Budget Cuts Demand a New Calculus," *Defense News*, July 31, 2020.

[4] LeMay Center for Doctrine Development and Education, *Annex 3-1 Department of the Air Force Role in Joint All-Domain Operations (JADO)*, June 1, 2020.

support this concept and maximize readiness will not be trivial; it requires preemptive consideration of supporting capabilities.

In response to an increasing need for joint training, a major line of effort in the *Air Force Operational Training Infrastructure [OTI] 2035 Flight Plan* is to strengthen joint interoperability with an objective of maximizing the ability to conduct frequent, relevant, and realistic joint training.[5] The use of the OTI plays a vital role in ensuring effective training and achieving warfighting dominance. As a key component of this infrastructure, live, virtual, and constructive (LVC) training capabilities can facilitate necessary training. LVC can help support the complex training JADC2 will require.[6] Use of LVC environments and instrumentation is one of seven focus points for the *Joint Operational Training Infrastructure Strategy*.[7] Thus, assessing specific training needs and processes and studying the extent to which LVC could improve training related to JADC2 needs, if at all, could help the USAF be proactive in supporting this new operational concept and preparing for the changing character of warfare.

This project investigates how LVC capabilities may help the USAF support the JADC2 initiative. The project supports the National Defense Strategy in meeting its objectives for rebuilding military readiness, particularly through addressing the development of leaders for future readiness requirements.[8] Within the USAF, current work on JADC2 focuses on the capabilities that air operations centers (AOCs) currently provide and primarily considers the air, cyber, and space domains. Thus, to facilitate forward-thinking investment strategies for LVC-related training, this project explores how the USAF executes the JADC2 concept for the AOC training audience, with a focus on training at tier 3 (service component) and tier 4 (unit and individual) levels. It is important to note that, as part of their operational tasks, AOC staff interact with systems and warfighters outside the AOC environment, and these external elements may necessitate simulation in an LVC training context. Although we explore the training process for AOC personnel from beginning to end, the explicit focus of this project was on continuation training (CT).

This report is intended for multiple audiences: the operational test and training infrastructure (OTTI) community in the Air Force, especially those whose interest lies in the domain of modeling and simulation; the Air Force community working with LVC and JADC2; and to some extent, the broader U.S. Department of Defense (DoD) training community. As noted above,

---

[5] Department of the Air Force, *Air Force Operational Training Infrastructure 2035 Flight Plan*, September 5, 2017, Not available to the general public.

[6] Note that we consider not just the complete integration of LVC capabilities but also the potential value of *blended* (live and virtual, or live and constructive) and *synthetic* (just virtual and/or constructive) aspects of LVC. These terms are explained in more detail in subsequent chapters of the report.

[7] Office of the Under Secretary of Defense for Personnel and Readiness, *Joint Operational Training Infrastructure Strategy*, March 2020.

[8] DoD, *Summary of 2018 National Defense Strategy of the United States of America: Sharpening the American Military's Competitive Edge*, 2018.

analyses concerning LVC and JADC2 have implications across the joint community. Furthermore, in the course of the study, we determined that a key element for facilitating efficient adoption of JADC2 is incorporating the end user as early and frequently as possible. Given the breadth of the JADC2 concept, the set of relevant end users spans more broadly than solely those personnel currently or formerly at AOCs. Thus, we wanted to ensure that readers unfamiliar with the operations of an AOC or with modeling and simulation generally also found this document accessible. In addition, even within the targeted USAF LVC community, there can be discrepancies in the meaning and scope of OTTI, LVC and its components, and nuances of AOC operations. Thus, the following background material provides a foundation with which to discuss the analysis.

Background

A key part of the evolution in warfighting depends on the operational capabilities constituted by test and training infrastructure, of which LVC is part.[9] Thus, just as it is important to consider the development of JADC2 in the context of trends in warfare, it is necessary to understand the training context, including OTI and OTTI. Broadly, OTI and OTTI refer to *technical* infrastructure that hosts, enables, and supports a holistic range of operational testing and training goals that are realistic, integrated, cross-domain, and explicitly supportive of training elements for air, space, and cyber.[10] As the concept of JADC2 develops, the OTI and OTTI take supportive roles, as do the LVC family of training modalities in OTI and OTTI. Here, we provide a brief overview of relevant concepts.

Defining LVC, OTI, and OTTI

Operational training and operational training infrastructure are defined as follows:[11]

- *Operational training*—mission-oriented training in support of warfighter readiness, distinguished from initial training by its focus on employment of a weapon system in an operational setting as opposed to basic use of equipment or development of basic skills
- *Operational training infrastructure*—technical infrastructure focused on warfighter readiness training and supporting systems, including training systems, live ranges,

---

[9] John R. Hoehn, *Joint All-Domain Command and Control (JADC2)*, Congressional Research Service, IF11493, version 15, July 1, 2021a; John R. Hoehn, *Joint All-Domain Command and Control: Background and Issues for Congress*, Congressional Research Service, R46725, version 8, August 12, 2021b; Alicia Datzman, "Joint All-Domain Command and Control Operational Success Requires Investment in Multi-Domain Test and Training," *Modern Integrated Warfare*, November 25, 2019.

[10] Air Force Instruction 99-103, Capabilities-Based Test and Evaluation, Department of the Air Force, November 18, 2019, additionally provides definitions for *operational testing* and *operational test and evaluation*, which are broader in scope and inclusive of organizational processes, personnel, and policy.

[11] Adapted from Air Force Instruction 16-1007, *Management of Air Force Operational Training Systems*, Department of the Air Force, October 1, 2019.

simulators, environment generators, threat emitters, aggressors, networks, training centers, and multidomain C2 training systems.[12]

OTI includes training-related technical infrastructure assets and supporting systems, such as facilities, networks, data systems, simulators, integration software, and performance measurement systems that are applied in support of force training.[13] Although OTI does include simulation and simulators—the synthetic aspects of training associated with LVC training—it is not limited to LVC.

The concept of OTTI extends OTI and integrates the technical infrastructure for *test* and training assets to enable realistic and relevant environments that also support testing of weapon systems and warfighter readiness training.[14] Using USAF usage of terms related to test and training environments, we define OTTI as follows:[15]

- *Operational test and training infrastructure*—technical infrastructure that combines test and training assets to enable realistic and relevant environments supporting operational testing of weapon systems and warfighter readiness training.

OTTI represents a shift away from the perspective that weapon systems, test infrastructure, and training infrastructure can all be developed independently of one another. Rather than necessarily promoting better training and better testing, the current acquisition, testing, and training approaches, in which training and testing are considered relatively late in the acquisition life cycle, can present risks to missions and force readiness. Thus, the OTTI concept intends to "break" the paradigm of "weapons system first, test and training infrastructure second."[16]

Operational test and training systems may rely on the same basic infrastructure to achieve weapon system testing goals and enable operational training. Thus, OTTI will bring together key intelligence, test, and training communities to promote holistic and relevant environments for test and training. In addition, test and training infrastructure assets will essentially combine and factor in the design stage of future weapon systems.

Simultaneously, there is the opportunity to improve the total cost and availability of test and training infrastructure for future weapon systems. That is, with its expanded emphasis on test and experimentation, OTTI can facilitate real-world implementation of technology and help highlight

---

[12] Although not explicitly noted in the literature, OTI can include human capital and workforce.

[13] Department of the Air Force, 2017.

[14] Joe Moschellam, "AFMC ACC OTTI TASR Briefs—ACC Operational Test & Training Infrastructure (OTTI)," Air Force Materiel Command Air Combat Command, January 30, 2020; Rick Jaime and Steve Trnka, "AFMC ACC OTTI TASR Briefs—ACC Operational Test & Training Infrastructure (OTTI) Acquisition Approach," Air Force Materiel Command Air Combat Command, January 29, 2020. Multiple objectives for the OTI enterprise, as described in Department of the Air Force, 2017, discuss both test and training as part of a single infrastructure or environment.

[15] The RAND-proposed definition is based on usage of terms related to test and training environments in Moschellam, 2020; Jaime and Trnka, 2020; and Department of the Air Force, 2017.

[16] Moschellam, 2020; Jaime and Trnka, 2020; and Department of the Air Force, 2017.

potential issues earlier in the acquisition process. Viewing test and training infrastructure capabilities alongside, and on equal footing with, the development of future weapon systems will enable the force to be ready for the future threats motivating the JADC2 concept. Warfighter training will keep pace with emerging capabilities on relevant time scales and at a level of operational effectiveness required for the future fight.

The different components of LVC, as well as the overall concept, provide key aspects of OTI and OTTI. Using an aggregation of various documents, we use the following definitions for LVC elements:[17]

- *Live simulation*—a simulation involving real people operating real weapon systems but without a live enemy. Although the term *live simulation* may seem like an oxymoron, it is common in the literature and constitutes a simulation because it simulates warfare without applying lethal force.
- *Virtual simulation*—a simulation involving real people operating simulated systems. Virtual simulations inject human-in-the-loop in a central role by exercising motor control skills (i.e., flying an airplane), decision skills (i.e., committing fire control resources to action), or communication skills (i.e., indicating the location of a target).
- *Constructive simulation*—a simulation involving computer-generated entities whereby simulated people operate simulated systems. A constructive simulation is a computer program. Real people may provide inputs to such simulations, but they are not involved in determining the outcomes.

Although these three independent aspects are well defined, the more general idea of LVC as an overall construct can sometimes spur confusion. Depending on the context, it is not always clear if the use of the term implies (1) the full integration of LVC simulation concurrently or (2) any use of synthetic training elements in which the term *synthetic* implies the use of virtual and/or constructive elements. *Blended* training refers to the combination of live training with virtual or constructive elements.[18] LVC elements are commonly used to support training, including distributed training and large-scale training exercises.

Furthermore, discussions of LVC can sometimes erroneously imply extension beyond just simulation capabilities and include a broader enterprise similar to OTI. Nonetheless, given JADC2's substantial changes in the way the USAF, and more generally DoD, may integrate and operate, LVC methods may offer the capabilities to match the scale and complexity of the operations that the JADC2 concept is meant to address.

---

[17] Defense Modeling and Simulation Enterprise, "M&S Glossary," U.S. Department of Defense, March 19, 2014; Air Force Instruction 16-1005, *Modeling and Simulation Management*, Department of the Air Force, June 23, 2016; Air Force Instruction 16-1007, 2019.

[18] Defense Modeling and Simulation Enterprise, 2014, describes a *war game* as a simulation game for which *constructive simulation* is a synonym.

Given the need to provide appropriate training for JADC2, one must also consider the training audience—the end users with whom JADC2 will be deployed. In practice, the conceptual shifts in C2 constructs, which are central to JADC2, will likely center on the heart of operational C2 in the USAF: the AOC.[19] This section provides an overview of the AOC, how it is structured, and how it operates.

Fundamentally, an AOC is a command center. The AOC weapon system, often termed the *Falconer system*, is a system of systems that incorporates multiple software applications.[20] It generally enables C2 of joint theater air and missile defense; multidomain target engagement operations; and intelligence, surveillance, and reconnaissance (ISR) operations management.[21] It is normally employed by the Joint Force Air Component Commander (JFACC) to exercise control of air forces in support of combined and joint force objectives.

Today, seven geographic AOCs and five global AOCs are located around the world, as detailed in Appendix D. Global AOCs support functional combatant commands (CCMDs) in the areas of global strike, mobility, space, special operations, and cyber. Geographic AOCs support geographic CCMDs and the planning and execution of theater operations in support of the joint force commander.[22]

The technology underlying the AOC is a web of C2 software systems that enables all phases of the air tasking cycle, which is a nominally 72-hour cycle that provides orders and documentation to translate an airpower strategy from the operational to the tactical level.[23] The cycle begins with the Strategy Division of the AOC defining objectives, effects, and guidance for the air tasking order (ATO) period. An ATO is essentially a detailed flying schedule. Given its current centrality, it is helpful to have a basic understanding of an ATO's status quo form to better consider how it may change to facilitate JADC2.[24]

---

[19] Theresa Hitchens, "From 'Mad Hatter' to 'Torque': Kessel Run Makes Software for F-22, CV-22," *Breaking Defense*, July 21, 2020c.

[20] The AOC is designated as the AN/USQ-163 Falconer weapon system. The designation as a weapon system helps drive proper management and standardization of the system, beginning with the designation of a lead command and program executive officer (PEO) for the system.

[21] Defense Acquisition Management Information Retrieval, *2016 Major Automated Information System Annual Report, Air and Space Operations Center-Weapon System Increment 10.2*, March 2016.

[22] Sherrill Lingel, Jeff Hagen, Eric Hastings, Mary Lee, Matthew Sargent, Matthew Walsh, Li Ang Zhang, and David Blancett, *Joint All-Domain Command and Control for Modern Warfare: An Analytic Framework for Identifying and Developing Artificial Intelligence Applications*, RAND Corporation, RR-4408/1-AF, 2020, p. 2.

[23] See Contingency and Crisis Execution: The Tasking Cycle in Air Force Doctrine Publication 3-0, Operations and Planning, Department of the Air Force, November 4, 2016, p. 116.

[24] Per the USAF, an ATO is a "method used to task and disseminate to components, subordinate units, and command and control agencies projected sorties, capabilities, and/or forces to targets and specific missions" (Joint Publication 3-30, *Joint Air Operations, Joint Chiefs of Staff*, July 25, 2019, p. GL-6).

The air tasking cycle is a personnel-intensive and deliberate cycle of coordination in which targets are developed, platforms are chosen to maximize probability of success and minimize risk, and legal and commander reviews are incorporated at multiple points.[25] Figure 1.1 illustrates some of the complexity of this process.[26] The continuous nature of the air tasking cycle means that as the Combat Operations Division is executing and monitoring a given day's ATO, the Combat Plans Division is planning the next day's ATO, and the Strategy Division is making preparations for the subsequent day (see Figure 1.1).

In recent years, the USAF has pursued technologies to enable the AOC to access information across domains as rapidly as possible. Although capabilities from air, space, maritime, ground, and cyber domains all contribute to military operations today, it is still difficult and time-consuming for AOCs to synthesize information across domains and to rapidly understand the environment and inform C2 decisionmaking. The process is primarily manual and is accomplished through coordination meetings, and despite inherent inefficiencies, it is doctrinally how the USAF integrates other domains.[27]

Figure 1.1. ATO Cycle

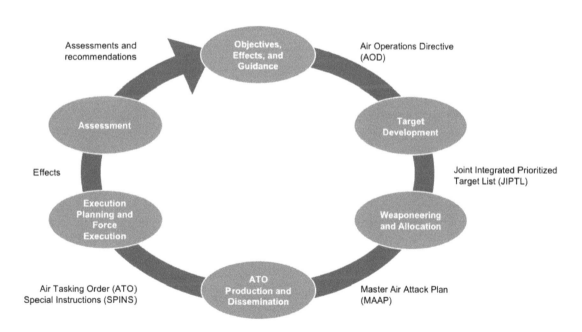

SOURCE: Adapted from Lingel et al., 2020.

---

[25] Lingel et al., 2020, p. 4.

[26] See Lingel et al., 2020, and Air Operations Center in Air Force Doctrine Publication 3-30, Command and Control, Department of the Air Force, January 7, 2020, for more detail.

[27] Air Force Doctrine Publication 3-30, Appendix B, 2020.

The AOC's current emphasis on deliberate planning and intensive personnel coordination to generate the ATO may be too slow for today's technological environment, in which decisions may need to be made in seconds.[28] Difficulties sharing information across classification levels and on multiple *air-gapped systems* (those that are physically disconnected from networks) also pose a challenge.[29] Other limitations to decision speed and cross-domain coordination are related to authorities, command relationships, disparate processes and battle rhythms across domains, varied C2 structures in different regions, and communications difficulties.[30]

Moreover, as we describe later in the report, much of the initial C2 training in the USAF is classroom focused, and training plans are not well aligned with developing JADC2 capabilities. Although USAF C2 training organizations are closely tracking technological shifts relevant to JADC2 (including the move to the Block 20 solutions at AOCs[31] and the introduction of Advanced Battle Management System [ABMS] and Kessel Run applications), their training plans do not yet consider these changes. Finally, C2 training in general is not being guided by a coherent vision of JADC2 that clearly explains why and how airmen should command and control forces across domains.[32]

Testing exercises, which are a part of CT at the AOCs, do offer some opportunity for gaining operational to tactical-level C2 training and experience and exposure to cross-domain C2 concepts. This is particularly true of the Exercises BLUE FLAG and VIRTUAL FLAG.[33] Although these exercises are internal to the USAF, the squadrons that manage them do seek joint and coalition participation to bring an element of cross-domain C2 realism to events.

However, although these exercises offer some experience of cross-domain C2 realism, their focus is on current practice rather than exploring JADC2 implementation. Moreover, training events that focus on C2 and AOC training are not frequent. In effect, this means that opportunities for the USAF to practice and fine-tune potentially pertinent concepts, such as distributed or decentralized C2, with the AOC as a specific training audience are relatively infrequent as well. Moreover, few exercises enable the full AOC to exercise every aspect of the air tasking cycle for similar reasons.

---

[28] Lingel et al., 2020, p. viii.

[29] Lingel et al., 2020, p. viii.

[30] Lingel et al., 2020, p. viii; Miranda Priebe, Douglas C. Ligor, Bruce McClintock, Michael Spirtas, Karen Schwindt, Caitlin Lee, Ashley L. Rhoades, Derek Eaton, Quentin E. Hodgson, and Bryan Rooney, *Multiple Dilemmas: Challenges and Options for All-Domain Command and Control*, RAND Corporation, RR-A381-1, 2020; 505th Command and Control Wing official, discussion with the authors, November 25, 2020.

[31] *Block 20 solutions* refer to AOC weapon systems that are in development and will replace the current Block 10 solutions.

[32] 505th Command and Control Wing (CCW) officials, discussion with the authors, December 16, 2020; 505th CCW officials, discussion with the authors, November 20, 2020; 505th CCW officials, discussion with the authors, November 25, 2020.

[33] These exercises are hosted by 505th CCW squadrons and serve as important opportunities for gaining operational to tactical-level C2 training and experience. They are also discussed in further detail in Chapter 3.

Objectives and Scope

The primary objective of this study was to explore how the OTI environment and LVC training systems might assist the USAF in supporting the development and execution of the JADC2 concept through training of AOC personnel in an effort to address the challenges and gaps discussed above.[34] Given this intent, the overarching questions we sought to answer were as follows:

- What are the primary training needs with respect to anticipated requirements for JADC2 across AOCs?
- What are the current processes and curricula for CT at AOCs?
- What LVC capabilities are available or under development that could help support training related to JADC2?
- How can the USAF leverage LVC to train for JADC2 most effectively?

Note that there was no initial assumption that LVC capabilities would or could enhance training for JADC2; exploring the value proposition for LVC in the JADC2 context was an overarching goal.

A few considerations help define the scope of this work. First, an inherent challenge in determining how to train for JADC2 is that the JADC2 concept is not yet fully developed. Therefore, we consider primarily the *current* plans for JADC2 and in some cases consider variations of anticipated outcomes (e.g., potential future distributed AOC structures). Second, although we focus on training, we do draw some conclusions concerning the ongoing development of JADC2 and propose related recommendations. Third, we focus primarily on CT, but we do note how initial qualification training (IQT) can help foster coordinated training practices. Finally, this is a study for the USAF on a topic that is inherently joint and thus relates to other services, so although we do note ongoing related efforts across DoD, we focus on determining how the USAF, in particular, can help support JADC2.

Approach

The overarching approach involved first assessing and aligning training requirements with LVC-related training capabilities across the operational AOCs. Then, given an understanding of what is needed to be trained and what technologies were available to address such needs, we evaluated the current training curricula and processes across the AOCs in an effort to understand the context in which LVC capabilities might be deployed. This approach is founded in the contention that training solutions must derive from and map to the training objectives. Much of

---

[34] Note that training for AOC staff involves warfighters and systems outside the AOC, some at the tactical edge. AOC staff are responsible for communicating with and interacting with personnel across echelons, domains, and services. Thus, although the focus of this work is on AOC staff, the potential benefits of LVC-related capabilities are assessed in the context of C2 that potentially integrates with personnel outside the AOCs.

this information was captured in a summary matrix looking at training needs, capabilities, and processes across the AOCs, which in turn highlighted any gaps, lessons learned, and/or duplicate effort. This overall approach was informed primarily by literature reviews and subject-matter expert (SME) interviews.

Between December 2020 and September 2021, we spoke to a variety of interlocutors. Various stakeholders are vital to understanding training requirements, identifying relevant capabilities, and potentially inserting LVC capabilities, and the team targeted these stakeholders for interviews and solicitation of relevant documentation. More specifically, we spoke to SMEs working with C2 at the various geographic and global AOCs to get a sense of the status quo and how they anticipated it might change to accommodate JADC2. We also spoke with SMEs about providing training for the AOCs, including at the 505th Training Squadron (TRS) and at Shadow Operations Center-Nellis (ShOC-N). We spoke to other stakeholders in the Air Force, joint community, and other services to develop a better understanding of what the JADC2 "job" would entail at the operational level from the USAF perspective. These stakeholders included contacts at Joint Staff (JS) J6, JS J7, and the Under Secretary of Defense for Research and Engineering. Finally, we spoke with SMEs from the science and technology community to gain a sense of anticipated technology and its potential implementation, both from an operational perspective and from the perspective of the training community, including the Kessel Run Experimentation Lab, ShOC-N, and the Air Force Research Laboratory. We conducted 50 interviews (often with multiple contacts from a given organization) from 44 different organizations, including subordinate units (for example, we interviewed personnel from multiple AF/A3T offices).

These interviews focused on three primary areas, related to our three primary tasks: what the JADC2 job would entail, or *determining the training needs* (e.g., software systems); what the *current training processes* were to determine what the status quo was and what was currently being done to accommodate JADC2; and what *technological capabilities* were currently available or under development. Although our approach focused primarily on the air domain given our sponsor, we also specifically explored developments for the cyber and space domains. Our interviews with personnel from other services had a slightly different orientation, given that we wanted to assess potential interoperability with the USAF rather than solely their approach to JADC2. We assessed what their efforts were toward implementing JADC2 and which organizations have primary responsibilities for those efforts; the current extent of collaboration with the Air Force, or with other services, regarding JADC2; their perceptions of how the USAF might support the given service for JADC2, and considerations regarding training posture necessary to implement JADC2.

We supplemented these interviews with literature reviews, reviews of job analysis or task list information where applicable, reviews of C2 task lists and other AOC documentation, and a review of the current state of the science of LVC and its applications for training. Specifically, to identify training needs and requirements for JADC2, we consulted official USAF publications;

secondary literature on joint- and multidomain C2; simulation-based training;[35] and a series of interviews with Department of the Air Force (DAF) and DoD officials involved in C2, training, and modeling and simulation. Our consideration of training processes included examination of a variety of published materials from DoD, including Air Force instructions, manuals, and policy guidance; individual AOC training plans; and Joint Staff documentation on training exercises. For consideration of technical capabilities, we reviewed DAF and DoD training and technology road maps published between 2016 and 2021, literature reviews of the current state of the art of LVC tools and technology, documentation on AOC systems, and relevant DoD research and development (R&D) program information and guidance.

In general, as we explored the use of LVC for training JADC2, we connected capabilities and processes back to training requirements identified early in the study. In addition, we identified opportunities for leveraging LVC most effectively. This culminated in a summary for how LVC can be leveraged for training in support of JADC2. Naturally, over the course of the study, the direction of JADC2, as well as supporting systems, shifted and matured; this evolution continues. Nonetheless, the analysis and consequent recommendations apply at a relatively high level and remain relevant.

Overview of the Report

The subsequent chapters in this report reflect the phases of the approach outlined above. Chapter 2 focuses on assessing training needs. We review the anticipated characteristics of warfare and how they map to JADC2 requirements, then derive training requirements related to JADC2. Drawing on our assessment of training needs, Chapter 3 offers a review of current training processes at AOCs. This includes an analysis of current and future AOC structure. Chapter 4 offers reviews and analyses of the current state of the art of LVC. This includes a review of capabilities that could support C2 training, a new framework for discussing information technology (IT) in support of JADC2, an assessment of distributed training systems that could support JADC2, and a summary of risks and issues concerning the cyber and space domains. Chapter 5 presents a matrix of training needs, processes and curricula, and capabilities across all AOCs with a discussion of gaps and seams. In addition, this chapter summarizes how LVC can be deployed to support JADC2 training. Chapter 6 provides a summary of findings and recommendations.

---

[35] For the literature review, we searched for related terms in Congressional Research Service, Defense Technical Information Center, and Google Scholar, and we snowballed additional references from references found in this process.

Chapter 2. Assessing Training Needs

In this chapter, we examine the impetus for developing a new C2 construct and the implications for anticipated training needs (objectives, goals, and requirements). To set the stage for an assessment of training requirements associated with JADC2, we first review the motivation for JADC2 itself. In this chapter, we ask (1) how future changes in the conduct of warfare will affect C2, (2) what JADC2 should entail in light of those changes, and (3) what will most likely be required to train and execute missions under JADC2.

As a concept geared toward addressing high-end conflict—for example, contingencies involving a confrontation with China over Taiwan—we begin by taking stock of likely changes in the technologies and conduct of warfare and the implications those changes have for C2 of U.S. military forces. We then describe what JADC2 should entail, drawing on the review of future changes in warfare and present implications for JADC2 operational and training requirements.

Factors That Drive Training Needs

A primary motivation of JADC2 is the changing nature of the threats that the U.S. military may face as envisioned by the most recent National Defense Strategy. As one U.S. Indo-Pacific Command (INDOPACOM) official involved in operational training observed, what is motivating JADC2 is that new threats demand that the Air Force move from decision to action more quickly than adversaries, and achieving this requires interoperability of tactical effects through strategic C2 networks across the services.[36]

Potential Changes in the Conduct of Warfare

Anticipated changes in the conduct of warfare and the emergence of new and enhanced military capabilities motivate the need for new C2 capabilities.[37] Figure 2.1 illustrates how these anticipated changes serve as a demand signal for the C2 capabilities that JADC2 intends to provide. Below, we describe how the connections in the figure are made, ordered by the relevant aspect of future warfare. Note that this does not represent an exhaustive analysis of how the conduct of warfare will change in the future, nor does it represent all the ways in which these changes motivate JADC2; rather, the focus is on specific aspects of JADC2 that are relevant to AOC operations.

---

[36] AOC official, interview with authors, January 28, 2021.

[37] For an overview of anticipated changes in the conduct of warfare, see John D. Winkler, Timothy Marler, Marek N. Posard, Raphael S. Cohen, and Meagan L. Smith, *Reflections on the Future of Warfare and Implications for Personnel Policies of the U.S. Department of Defense*, RAND Corporation, PE-324-OSD, 2019.

Figure 2.1. How Anticipated Changes in Warfare Drive the Development of JADC2

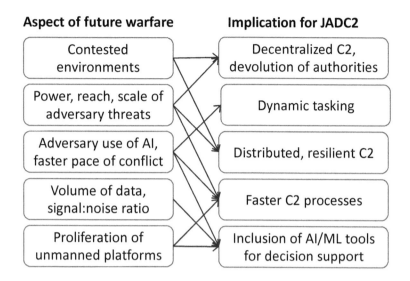

NOTE: AI = artificial intelligence; ML = machine learning.

Near-peer adversaries, such as China and Russia, can bring to bear many capabilities that the U.S. military has not confronted in recent military engagements, including anti-access and area denial (A2/AD) capabilities. *Adversary A2/AD capabilities* can deny U.S. forward forces the ability to maintain connectivity to centralized C2 nodes. Thus, C2 in any near-peer conflict scenario would be contested in a manner that demands new concepts and capabilities, including the ability to distribute C2 nodes. Distributing C2 nodes across space helps ensure that the ability to exercise C2 in a given mission does not depend on the survival of one central node, for instance, on an AOC.[38] Distributing C2 nodes across space increases the resiliency of the larger C2 network in contested environments.[39]

A2/AD capabilities also place a premium on the ability to *decentralize* C2. We adopt a usage of decentralized C2 that is distinct from *distributed* C2; we use the latter to indicate the physical distribution of C2 *capabilities* across space, whereas we use the former to indicate the decentralization of C2 *authorities*.[40] Under a decentralized C2 concept, C2 authorities would be

---

[38] Gilmary M. Hostage III and Larry R. Broadwell, Jr., "Resilient Command and Control: The Need for Distributed Control," *Joint Force Quarterly*, Vol. 74, July 2014.

[39] Air Force Lessons Learned, *Doolittle Series 18: Multi-Domain Operations*, Air University Press, LeMay Papers, Vol. 3, 2019.

[40] Decentralization and distribution are used interchangeably in some literature, see for example, Stefan Morell, "Optimizing Joint All-Domain C2 in the Indo-Pacific," *Air and Space Power Journal*, Summer 2021. We adopt a distinction because the two concepts do not necessarily overlap along all relevant dimensions. For example, C2 authorities assigned to a given organization and command level, such as an AOC, may be distributed but not decentralized if a given AOC is distributed across space; those same authorities may be both distributed and decentralized if they are handed off to a different command level based on a set of contingencies.

passed to lower command echelons—that is, *local* C2—under a certain set of prespecified conditions.[41] For example, C2 authorities could be handed off to an Airborne Warning and Control System—an airborne C2 platform—when conditions indicate that an AOC may soon lose the ability to exercise centralized C2 over a mission. The ability to hand off C2 authorities to another level ensures that tactical forces can continue to execute their mission during a period in which connectivity to centralized nodes is lost.

Of course, near-peer capabilities have implications for more than just C2. More generally, the **greater power, reach, and scale of near-peer capabilities**—for example, long-range strike and highly capable ISR assets—mean that future conflicts will likely overrun traditional areas that have defined the operational boundaries of geographic CCMDs.[42] Greater adversary capability has the same implications as above for distributed and decentralized C2. If near-peer adversaries can generate sufficient standoff, the ability of forward forces to exercise C2 at a local level becomes more important. Distributed and decentralized C2 capabilities can allow forward forces to execute their mission under such circumstances. For example, sophisticated adversary ISR capabilities place a premium on keeping communications between rear and forward forces to a minimum while enabling local C2.[43]

The **speed and range of adversary capabilities**—to include A2/AD capabilities—imply a need for C2 concepts and capabilities that allow dynamic tasking that is responsive to rapidly changing tactical and operational scenarios. Such scenarios may arise due to a high-velocity weapon crossing areas of responsibility (AORs), where commanders in different AORs may need sensors from other domains or under other commands to effectively execute missile defense.[44]

The increasing sophistication of ISR capabilities means that the future battlefield will be awash with **greater volumes of data** that must somehow be organized to facilitate decisionmaking. Merging data from multiple sources may increase or decrease the **noise to signal ratio**, depending on the choice of data sources and related analytic techniques. The proliferation of ISR sensors across domains—from maritime sensors to sensors aboard fighter aircraft to low-earth orbit satellites—and the potential relevance of data from commercial applications will demand the capability to fuse and process massive amounts of data to accelerate decisionmaking.[45] Even with the ability to ingest and store large volumes of data, C2 organizations need appropriate tools to sift through, fuse, and analyze that data to filter out noise

---

[41] For information on different constructs to enable decentralized C2, see Priebe et al., 2020.

[42] Winkler et al., 2019.

[43] DAF officials, interview with authors, March 25, 2021.

[44] Theresa Hitchens, "MDA: All-Domain C2 Key to Countering Hypersonic Missiles," *Breaking Defense*, May 14, 2020b.

[45] Winkler et al., 2019.

and provide the relevant information to the right decisionmaker.[46] One final possibility is that some of the data generated for use in and by LVC applications could be used to generate fake data (e.g., sensor tracks) to overwhelm adversaries' ability to decide and act. All of this requires the development of AI/ML applications and their insertion at the right points throughout the C2 process.[47]

Adversaries will employ AI/ML applications in their own C2 processes for the same purpose of **accelerating their own decision cycles**. In addition to new capabilities, such as hypersonic weapons, these capabilities are likely to drive an increase in the pace of conflict and an ability to reduce the time between decisions.[48] China, for example, is considering the use of AI at the tactical levels of warfare up through strategic levels.[49] AI/ML tools also enable U.S. and **adversary use of unmanned platforms** to operate independently or in man-machine teams. The use of unmanned platforms alongside AI/ML applications that enable rapid, coordinated behavior (e.g., swarms of small drones) demand extremely fast C2 capabilities to counter such threats.[50]

These shifts in the conduct of warfare will require that C2 tools, processes, and personnel adapt. The necessary adaptations will likely represent changes in degree and not in kind: The military is used to coordinating effects across domains but will need to do so faster (potentially at greater-than-human speed).[51] The military must be prepared to manage C2 when communications are contested and reliance on distributed C2 nodes is necessary. DoD currently fuses data from a variety of sensors but will need to do so with more data, incorporate greater automation, and do so more quickly.[52] These shifts in warfare in part motivate the need for new C2 concepts like JADC2.

Characteristics of JADC2

The evolving trends in warfare require a new operational concept so that the United States remains competitive against future adversaries. JADC2 is a primary response to these trends; in this section, we summarize the overarching goals of JADC2; potential JADC2 requirements; and the roles, responsibilities, and interactions among the military services in support of JADC2.

---

[46] AOC official, interview with authors, May 11, 2021.

[47] For an analysis of where AI/ML applications may fit within Air Force C2 processes, see Lingel et al., 2020.

[48] Winkler et al., 2019.

[49] For information on China's approach to the use of AI in command control, see Elsa B. Kania, "Battlefield Singularity: Artificial Intelligence, Military Revolution, and China's Future Military Power," Center for a New American Security, November 2017.

[50] For information on unmanned platforms and consequences for C2, see Michael C. Horowitz, "When Speed Kills: Lethal Autonomous Weapon Systems, Deterrence and Stability," *Journal of Strategic Studies*, Vol. 42, No. 6, 2019.

[51] DAF official, interview with authors, January 28, 2021.

[52] AOC official, interview with authors, May 11, 2021.

JADC2 Goals

At a very basic level, JADC2 represents an attempt to change the way DoD fights and support that change with appropriate organizational structure and technology. Discussions of JADC2 often focus on the goal of **linking every sensor to every shooter**, such that the most appropriate platform is chosen to generate a desired effect, regardless of domain.[53] The JADC2 concept aims to **deliver a more general set of capabilities to support faster and more-accurate decisionmaking**; in support of this, it aims to **link tactical and strategic networks together to enable the fast ingestion, fusion, and transport of data across domains**.[54] The end goal is to **provide a decisionmaking advantage over near-peer adversaries by leveraging sensor data from all domains, automation tools, resilient networks, and distributed C2 structures**.[55]

JADC2 is more specifically aimed at supporting decisionmaking in high-end conflict. The ability to construct a common operating picture (COP) is central to operational planning and performing C2 of assets across multiple domains.[56] Given the speed of conflict and nature of threats that cross geographic areas and domains, JADC2 is meant to **enable dynamic tasking and retasking**, such that an appropriate course of action is produced as threats and opportunities rapidly change. In its current state, C2 processes across the air, space, and cyber domains are not set up to task assets dynamically; JADC2 is meant to address the silos and accelerate timelines for tasking across domains.[57]

Given that JADC2 is intended as a concept for high-end conflict, it should **enable resilient C2** in the face of adversaries' ability to contest and degrade the information and communication environments. Not only can near-peer adversaries disrupt and destroy communication nodes, they also can operate in a way that requires U.S. forces to operate at greater distances from the battlefield, making distributed C2 nodes more valuable.

Finally, the Air Force has explored different operating constructs for **executing C2 across domains**. Potential constructs include a restructuring of the AOC toward an organization that works across multiple domains (a multidomain operations center [MDOC]) or all domains (an all-domain operations center [ADOC]), as discussed in detail in Chapter 3.[58] Specifically, the Air Force is considering constructs to enable the passage of C2 authorities based on a prespecified set of conditions to continue mission execution in contested and degraded environments. Under

---

[53] See, for example, Hoehn, 2021a.

[54] DAF officials, interview with authors, January 28, 2021.

[55] Hoehn, 2021a.

[56] DAF officials, interview with authors, January 26, 2021.

[57] DAF officials, interview with authors, March 25, 2021.

[58] U.S. Air Force, *Air Force Future Operating Concept: A View of the Air Force in 2035*, Department of the Air Force, September 2015; DAF official, interview with authors, March 16, 2021.

this vision, commanders could pass mission-type orders to lower command echelons to enable forward units to exercise local C2 in accordance with a commander's intent.[59] To enable survivable C2 in high-end conflict, JADC2 will need to provide technologies to allow for the handoff and receipt of such authorities, both within and across command echelons.[60]

JADC2 Requirements

To achieve the JADC2 goals discussed above, including the ability to integrate across services, JADC2 requires a combination of automation tools, infrastructure, common data architectures, organizational and process changes, and training capabilities. As noted previously, automation tools, such as AI/ML algorithms, will be important for directing unmanned assets and enabling manned-unmanned teams. More generally, AI/ML tools will be necessary to process large amounts of authoritative data and make recommendations to human decisionmakers for courses of action. They may also be important for closing holes in disrupted networks by selecting C2 nodes through which to route communications in contested environments.[61]

There are dangers in potential uses of AI/ML tools for decision support in C2. Solutions that work in an artificial or training environment may fail in an unpredictable manner once used in a real operation. Because algorithms are likely to be trained on simulated data—a variety of potential operational use cases do not have large existing datasets on which to train, and security considerations will often require simulated data regardless—there is a risk that trainees might succeed in training simply by following algorithmic recommendations. Therefore, it is important that LVC testbeds be developed to verify and validate algorithms and place closed-form guardrails on their operation.

New data sharing capabilities will be central to JADC2. Consequently, networks with high bandwidth and low latency will be required to handle the large amounts of data that will contribute to the COP. Joint and service organizations will also need to adopt common data architectures and standards to enable seamless data sharing across domains and platforms. Given the need to coordinate across DoD, industry, civilian agencies, research institutions, and international partners,[62] implementing common data standards and enacting incentives for their

---

[59] Air Force Doctrine Publication 3-99, *Department of the Air Force Role in Joint All-Domain Operations (JADO)*, Department of the Air Force, October 8, 2020.

[60] See Air Force Doctrine Publication 1, *The Air Force*, Department of the Air Force, March 10, 2021; and Sandeep Mulgund, "Evolving the Command and Control of Airpower," *Wild Blue Yonder Online Journal*, April 21, 2021, for information on centralized command, distributed control, and decentralized execution.

[61] For information on communications dependence and multidomain operations, see Priebe et al., 2020.

[62] Theresa Hitchens, "OSD, Joint Staff Double Down on DoD-Wide Data Standards," *Breaking Defense*, February 10, 2021b.

testing and use could present a challenge.[63] Passing information across security levels is a necessity to realize the vision of JADC2 but represents a significant challenge for the services.[64] Beyond the services, JADC2 will require the ability to share data with partners and allies. Given that the concept is aimed at supporting high-end conflict, the United States is highly unlikely to make intensive use of JADC2 capabilities without some multinational participation.

JADC2 will likely require local data storage and processing capabilities to enable forward C2. This is a key enabling capability for enabling conditions-based authorities to be passed in the contested environments.[65] The degree to which these capabilities will be necessary to support JADC2 depends in part on which organizational concepts, such as MDOCs or ADOCs, the Air Force and DoD ultimately settle on.

Related to the above organizational concepts, JADC2 will also likely require new capabilities to enable commanders to leverage information from other domains to synchronize effects or deconflict fires. This will entail merging data streams from across domains into a COP that a commander can use to, for example, select the right effect for taking out an air defense system.[66] This will also entail efforts to identify and close gaps in how individual nodes communicate across domains, for instance, to make sure that pilot communications are understood by ground forces and commanders, where necessary.

Finally, JADC2 will require new training capabilities to match the scale and complexity of the operations that the concept is meant to address. Training for JADC2 will require the ability to simulate large numbers of entities, degraded and contested environments, and credible effects from all domains and from the tactical to strategic levels of war.[67] The use of AI/ML tools in C2 processes will require large amounts of data to train algorithms; these data could potentially be generated synthetically or otherwise collected from training environments.[68] As detailed later in the report, LVC can help with these training needs in various capacities.

The JADC2 requirements discussed above are summarized as follows and provide a reference point for our analysis of training processes and capabilities:

1. AI/ML tools for processing large amounts of data and making recommendations to decisionmakers
2. closed-form algorithms based on certifiable processes that provide guardrails for the AI/ML tools
3. operational networks with high bandwidth and low latency

---

[63] Timothy Marler, Matthew W. Lewis, Mark Toukan, Ryan Haberman, Ajay K. Kochhar, Bryce Downing, Graham Andrews, and Rick Eden, *Supporting Joint Warfighter Readiness: Opportunities and Incentives for Interservice and Intraservice Coordination with Training-Simulator Acquisition and Use*, RAND Corporation, RR-A159-1, 2021.

[64] Lingel et al., 2020; DAF officials, interview with authors, February 10, 2021.

[65] Navy officials, interview with authors, June 18, 2021.

[66] DAF officials, interviews with authors, March 16, 2021, and March 25, 2021.

[67] DAF officials, interview with authors, December 18, 2020.

[68] DAF officials, interviews with authors, August 18, 2021; Lingel et al., 2020, pp. 22–29.

4. common data architectures and standards
5. ability to pass data across multiple levels of security
6. ability to share data across services, partners, and allies
7. local data storage and processing capabilities that are furnished with appropriate zeroization[69] capabilities in the event capabilities fall into adversary hands
8. ability to merge data streams from across domains into a COP
9. large amounts of data that are classified with known classification labels to train ML algorithms for operational and training use.

Roles and Responsibilities

A fundamental aspect of the vision of JADC2 is to enable communication and dataflows across domains. Training will most likely feature novel interactions with other services at the operational and tactical levels. We provide a brief overview here of other services' relevant efforts to identify how they might inform the DAF's training posture for JADC2. See Appendix B for a more in-depth description of the specific offices involved in the development of JADC2 and the roles of the other services.

Given the joint nature of JADC2, it is critical to understand efforts under other services, their perceptions about DoD-wide integration, and how the Air Force can integrate most effectively. This helps inform Air Force plans for training for JADC2 from a joint perspective, which is especially critical given feedback from various SMEs that there is a need to train warfighters to think "jointly." To date, the services' concrete efforts toward JADC2 include the Air Force's ABMS program; the U.S. Army's Project Convergence, which involves a series of demonstrations to incorporate AI/ML tools into multidomain operations and more generally pursue joint and coalition interoperability; and the U.S. Navy's Project Overmatch, which is an effort at developing a tactical network that links sensors across domains.[70] Joint Modernization Command's JADC2 Division (under Army Futures Command) is leading the Project Convergence effort.[71] The Army intends to involve the Air Force and Navy in its Project Convergence 2021 exercise and involve multinational partners in 2022.[72]

---

[69] *Zeroization* is a "method of erasing electronically stored data, cryptographic keys, and credentials service providers (CSPs) by altering or deleting the contents of the data storage to prevent recovery of the data" (National Institute of Standards and Technology Computer Security Resource Center, "Glossary," undated).

[70] Given our Air Force focus, we did not explore the organizational details of other services' approach to JADC2 in as much detail.

[71] The Futures and Concepts Center and the Combat Capabilities Development Command's Command, Control, Communications, Computers, Cyber, Intelligence, Surveillance and Reconnaissance Center also support JADC2 and Project Convergence efforts.

[72] Andrew Feickert, *The Army's Project Convergence*, Congressional Research Service, IF11654, June 2, 2022.

Training Requirements

Given the goals and consequent requirements of JADC2 from an operational perspective, we now turn to translating the anticipated characteristics of JADC2 into actual training requirements. Given that JADC2 remains in development, it is not possible to specify what it will require for training *precisely*. However, the review of future changes in warfare, Air Force and DoD documentation, and interviews with key officials involved in the DAF's C2 training enterprise allow us to describe the contours of what will be required to support training for JADC2. Thus, in this section we first summarize the broad mission sets most relevant to JADC2 as high-level training requirements. We then translate anticipated JADC2 goals and requirements (discussed above) into training needs relevant specifically to AOCs. Finally, we review USAF doctrine and existing instructional programs for C2. In Appendix C, we also review the current training requirements process and related task lists and how they might be used to define training needs relevant to JADC2. One of our original aims with this overview was to define training requirements in which LVC might ultimately play a role. However, we uncovered general challenges to implementation of JADC2 in the training requirements process.

Relevant Missions

With its aim to draw together data from across domains into a common network, JADC2 has the potential to affect almost any mission; for example, a recent exercise that sought to develop JADC2 capabilities focused on logistics by tying together data from a variety of sources.[73] However, with the focus of JADC2 on enabling C2 in high-end conflict, primary missions include those that may occur in such scenarios, particularly those that may require the synchronization of effects across domains. For example, suppression of enemy air defenses (SEAD) is a mission that typically fell in the purview of the JFACC. With the development of Army long-range precision fires, the Army and Air Force are considering how to conduct C2 to execute SEAD missions using assets across the air, space, and ground domains.[74] JADC2 will further enhance other mission sets relevant to high-end conflict that already feature a multidomain aspect, such as close air support, integrated air and missile defense,[75] or missions with a strong time-sensitive element such as dynamic targeting or other ISR missions.[76]

---

[73] Patrick Tucker, "AI Gives 'Days of Advanced' Warning in Recent NORTHCOM Networked Warfare Experiment," *Defense One*, July 29, 2021.

[74] Joint Staff officials, interview with authors, June 2, 2021; Priebe et al., 2020, pp. 36–37.

[75] Priebe et al., 2020, pp. 67–76.

[76] DAF officials, interview with authors, February 10, 2021.

AOC-Specific Training Requirements

Because future military contingencies are likely to span AORs, AOCs will likely need to train to work alongside other AOCs that might have different operational rhythms and processes.[77] In this section, we view the anticipated goals and requirements of JADC2 (discussed above) through the lens of AOC personnel.

Training across AOCs and AORs will require networked training ranges to connect multiple training audiences.[78] Similarly, some AOC personnel will need **better understanding of the capabilities and effects that other domains can bring to bear**, for instance, how long it takes to move an asset from one place to another.[79] The ability to use capabilities from other domains will require experience incorporating those assets early in the planning process. For example, AOC personnel could train on incorporating cyber effects in the planning process and then simulating execution to learn about the effectiveness of planning cyber effects.[80] Effects from space and cyber in particular are difficult to include in training given that authorities often reside at the national level and the length of space and cyber planning cycles tend to be longer than planning cycles in the air domain.[81]

Requirements for **training alongside other AOCs and across command echelons** will depend on whether and to what degree DoD and the DAF pursue alternative command constructs like the MDOC or ADOC, among other potential changes. If these constructs are pursued, AOCs will need training capabilities to practice the handoff and receipt of operational C2 authorities. Experimentation and training will be needed to identify and practice the conditions under which C2 authorities could be passed down, for example, to the tactical level.[82] More generally, AOC personnel would need to be educated on which sorts of connectivity possibilities are available for continuing mission execution under complex, adverse conditions.[83]

Access to **operationally complex, high-threat training environments** is a requirement for training AOC personnel for almost any vision of JADC2 that is ultimately implemented. A common theme across discussions with AOC personnel and C2 training SMEs is that the most challenging aspects of operational environments are often *white-carded*, whereby an event in a training environment is briefed to trainees but not simulated by degraded communications or other challenges that necessitate recognition and action on the part of trainees. This is particularly true of simulation of contested and degraded environments. For example, AOC

---

[77] DAF officials, interview with authors, January 22, 2021.

[78] DAF officials, interview with authors, December 18, 2020.

[79] DAF officials, interview with authors, March 16, 2021.

[80] DAF officials, interviews with authors, February 10, 2021, and August 5, 2021.

[81] DAF official, interview with authors, August 27, 2021.

[82] Joint Staff officials, interview with authors, March 12, 2021.

[83] DAF officials, interview with authors, March 25, 2021.

personnel will need more-realistic training experience reacting to simulated attacks on their C2 infrastructure and determining the effects of simulated attacks on adversary infrastructure.[84] Electronic warfare (EW) is a notable operational training gap. Exercising against or with EW capabilities is rarely done, because (1) it can present security concerns and (2) it can be disruptive to commercial systems. LVC capabilities can provide additional capacity to exercise with and against EW capabilities either by using hardware in a secure facility or embedding EW capabilities in existing simulations.

The last set of potential training requirements focuses on **automation tools and interacting with large volumes of data** from a variety of sources, both classified and unclassified. AI/ML tools require habituation and user trust of the output of algorithms, as well as training on the proper use of data sources, including unclassified data. A synthesis of 27 years of organizational innovation research noted that a major but often unrecognized gap exists between the decision to implement an innovation and its actual implementation, and this issue is relevant here as well.[85] AOC personnel have expressed some skepticism of using AI-generated inputs to their operational processes; a new set of technical skills and practice with using these tools will be necessary for their incorporation into AOC processes.[86] Automated systems often increase the amount of training required to enable skilled personnel to intervene on the functioning of a complex system and maintain situational awareness.[87] Simulations may struggle to replicate the extreme circumstances under which human intervention in automated systems is necessary.[88]

Just as AOC personnel will require training on the use of AI/ML systems, they will also require simulation capabilities that represent adversary use of those same types of systems, a capability that is currently lacking for AOC C2 training.[89] JADC2 envisions the use of large amounts of data from a variety of new sources, potentially to include open-source, commercial, and unclassified data. AOC personnel may need training on the proper use of these data sources.[90]

A summary of AOC-specific training requirements follows:

- a better understanding of the capabilities and effects that other domains can bring to bear
- ability to train alongside other AOCs and across command echelons

---

[84] DAF officials, interview with authors, December 18, 2020.

[85] Mary M. Crossan and Marina Apaydin, "A Multi-Dimensional Framework of Organizational Innovation: A Systematic Review of the Literature," *Journal of Management Studies*, Vol. 47, No. 6, 2010.

[86] Lingel et al., 2020, pp. 44–45. The authors also note that AI systems that lack "explainable" output may impede the development of user trust.

[87] John K. Hawley, "PATRIOT WARS: Automation and the Patriot Air and Missile Defense System," Center for a New American Security, January 2017.

[88] Hawley, 2017.

[89] DAF official, interview with authors, December 16, 2020.

[90] DoD officials, interview with authors, April 23, 2021.

- familiarity with connectivity options, and receipt or delegation of nonstandard authorities for continuing mission execution under complex, adverse conditions
- ability to train in operationally complex, high-threat environments
- less reliance on white-carding
- training with automation tools and interacting with large volumes of data
- training against adversary use of AI/ML in C2 processes.

Doctrinal Considerations

Air Force doctrine details several considerations for JADC2 operations that focus on modifications to the traditional hierarchical C2 structure to allow more decentralized authority. This provides additional insight into training requirements to support JADC2. In general, the guidance set forth focuses on approaches that allow joint forces from across domains to work together efficiently and seamlessly. The driving factor behind this doctrine is the perceived importance of staying many steps ahead of a near-peer adversary.

Guidance for the Air Force's role in joint all-domain operations (JADO) and the vision for JADC2 were set forth as Air Force doctrine in 2020. In doctrine, JADC2 is described as the C2 vision for JADO and many of the outlined operating concepts align with the JADC2 goals discussed earlier in the chapter. In general, emphasis is placed on interconnectedness of assets, distributed operations, delegated authorities, and integrated planning across all domains.[91] The ultimate goal of JADO and by extension JADC2 is to enable the integration of effects across all domains to deter and defeat near-peer adversaries.[92] Doctrine outlines current operational gaps and provides general guidance on how the Air Force can support the development and implementation of the concepts summarized here.

JADC2 will necessitate **longer planning cycles**, which emphasize higher-level goals and rely on subordinate commanders to make adjustments as missions progress. Although producing some inefficiencies, these longer planning cycles can help mitigate the adverse impacts of degraded communications through extending subordinate autonomy.[93] Longer planning cycles can facilitate comprehension of mission, even while JADC2 capabilities should support quicker reaction cycles to emerging operational conditions. Doctrine emphasizes **delegated authority and decisionmaking** expectations for subordinate commanders. Even having a clear understanding of condition-based authorities may be insufficient because not all scenarios can be considered. Subordinates need to have a clear understanding of commander intent, so they can adapt and refine plans to meet mission objectives in any scenario.[94]

---

[91] Air Force Doctrine Publication 3-99, 2020.

[92] Air Force Doctrine Note 1-20, 2020.

[93] Air Force Doctrine Publication 3-99, 2020.

[94] Air Force Doctrine Note 1-20, 2020.

Developing a clear understanding of both **how to communicate and how to operate in situations in which communications are degraded** is essential. To communicate effectively, operators will need a solid understanding of the information systems in use. This includes basic operations as well as limitations of how systems used in different domains interface with each other. **A standardized lexicon** and **shared understanding of joint force capabilities and limitations** among joint forces are essential to streamlining processes and ensuring that everyone involved is on the same page. To fully realize the advantages of a joint all-domain effort, decisionmakers need to develop an in-depth understanding of the available capabilities.[95] As noted previously, C2 officers must have sufficient knowledge of the systems, processes, and capabilities used by the other services and joint partners so that joint planning efforts can be developed and implemented effectively.

Instructional Programs for C2

With training requirements derived from JADC2 goals and USAF doctrine as a foundation, this section focuses on instructional C2 programs and targeted skills that may support emerging JADC2 requirements. The U.S. Department of Education's National Center for Education Statistics developed a taxonomy for classifying instruction programs known as the Classification of Instructional Programs (CIP). This has been applied to education programs in many fields, including what O*NET[96] labels *Command and Control Center Officers*. This job field spans several operational C2 positions among is the new Air Force Specialty Code (13O) for Multi-Domain Warfare Officer, who are trained to be C2 experts specializing in joint operations planning across domains.[97] This career field was developed to alleviate some of the perceived capability gaps for implementation of multidomain warfare in the USAF,[98] and hence the related educational programs for it may yield useful insight regarding the focus of current training requirements.

O*NET defines the job responsibilities for Command and Control Center Officer positions as follows:[99]

> Manage the operation of communications, detection, and weapons systems
> essential for controlling air, ground, and naval operations. Duties include

---

[95] Air Force Doctrine Publication 3-99, 2020.

[96] O*NET is a national database of occupational data sponsored by the U.S. Department of Labor and Employment and Training Administrations. It is available online as a public resource for workforce data. It has been developed as a comprehensive source of real-world job information (including information on relevant knowledge, skills, and abilities) to foster an understanding of occupations generally as well as workforce impact on the U.S. economy.

[97] Since the time of writing, the 13O career field has been discontinued. However, this does not negate the utility of examining training programs for this career field, given the intent of the career field to develop multidomain C2 experts.

[98] Francisco Gallei, "Multi-Domain Warfare Officer, the 13O," *Air Land Sea Bulletin*, No. 2020-1, Winter 2020.

[99] O*NET Online, "Command and Control Center Officers," webpage, undated.

managing critical communication links between air, naval, and ground forces; formulating and implementing emergency plans for natural and wartime disasters; coordinating emergency response teams and agencies; evaluating command center information and need for high-level military and government reporting; managing the operation of surveillance and detection systems; providing technical information and advice on capabilities and operational readiness; and directing operation of weapons targeting, firing, and launch computer systems.

Descriptions for the seven educational program categories related to the development of C2 officer skills are given in more detail in Appendix A. The programs focus on the skills needed to perform in a C2 center, such as an AOC. Content areas in these programs cover the following topics, which reflect specific training needs for C2 officers and for JADC2 in general:

- information systems
- communications
- operations management
- planning
- information security
- decisionmaking
- doctrine and policy.

Across the programs, there is a heavy technical emphasis, which focuses on information systems, communications, and information security. Content includes C2 weapon system operations; global, local, and wireless networking; computing; cyber and space effects; and satellite communications. Gaining mastery over the technical environment is imperative for efficient functioning in a C2 center. With the inclusion of content on cyber and space effects, operators in training will be able to better understand how to operate beyond the air domain and coordinate a wider variety of specialized effects.

In addition to the technical content, there is also a focus on developing the procedural and behavioral skills necessary for successfully working in a C2 role. Effectively managing and planning operations requires the ability to maintain situational awareness and make informed decisions. Combined with the technical expertise to interact with and use C2 weapon systems, these training programs are intended to produce operators capable of conducting C2 across warfighting domains. O*NET is a resource for the general U.S. workforce rather than the military; it does not directly collect detailed information on military occupations. Because of this, the C2 officer job category covers several career fields that share a common focus on C2. The instructional programs linked to these occupations are courses found in officer training programs, and they provide an indication of the C2 emphasis for young officers. Although these programs do not describe AOC-specific training, they provide an overview of the educational background that officers may bring with them to the AOCs.

The ATO Process

All AOCs engage in the development and dissemination of ATOs as illustrated in Figure 1.1. Hence, their production constitutes a significant training need. Examination of this training need presents a different perspective from which to consider insertion of LVC into the training process. The quantity of ATOs produced and the duration of the ATO process vary depending on the primary mission and nature of each AOC. A typical AOC will have five divisions, each of which play a role in the ATO process at different stages. Table 2.1 lists the role of each division in the ATO process. Traditionally, the ATO cycle involves a 72-hour development phase, at the end of which, the ATO is produced along with any special instructions, and the mission is executed.

Table 2.1. AOC Division Contributions to the ATO Process

Division	Role
Strategy	Provides high-level guidance on air operations to meet objectives
Combat plans	Produces the MAAP and ATO
Combat operations	Produces daily ATO changes
ISR	Conducts ISR operations and provides target acquisition information to the ATO
Air mobility	Plans and executes air mobility and provides air apportionment plans to MAAP and ATO

SOURCE: Adapted from Air Force Doctrine Publication 3-30, Appendix B: The Air Operation Center, 2020.
NOTE: MAAP = master air attack plan.

Using a review of the ATO stages, we identified basic work functions that AOC staff are likely to engage in throughout the ATO cycle. Appendix E outlines the general stages of the ATO process and lists basic work functions that underlie each stage. Under JADC2, the overall structure of the ATO process is unlikely to change significantly. However, in each stage of the process, the basic work functions are likely to be affected by JADC2 and thus represent relevant and specific training needs. As the actual work to perform basic functions changes, modifications to the training process will be needed. Table 2.2 lists basic work functions involved in the ATO process and specifies how each of them might be affected under JADC2. These basic work functions reflect specific training needs to support C2 and JADC2.

Table 2.2. Basic AOC Work Functions and Potential Impacts Under JADC2

Basic Work Function	Potential Impact of JADC2
Data analysis	Increased automation and built-in guidance
Data management	Increased integration with various data sources; streamlined storage and retrieval
Decisionmaking	Readily available comprehensive information; enhanced decision support tools, guidance, and modeling of outcomes
Deconfliction	Increased automation; integration of data across services and domains
Information-gathering	Increased efficiency through a network of connected sensors

Basic Work Function	Potential Impact of JADC2
Information-sharing	Increased integration across systems, domains, and services
Writing	Increased automation
Development	Extensive increases in automation, data accessibility, and streamlined procedures to decrease the amount of time from the beginning of the ATO cycle to ATO execution

The manner in which AOC staff are trained on the ATO process varies depending on AOC resources and needs and an individual's role in a particular AOC (discussed in greater detail in Chapter 3). Ultimately, AOCs need flexibility to train any and all aspects of the ATO process in a variety of training contexts. LVC technology can help fill potential gaps and provide more opportunities for division- and individual-focused training. Using LVC, training can be implemented independently or in parallel with a large-scale training exercise. In these contexts, LVC provides a framework for simulating ideal and degraded conditions providing more-dynamic and more-realistic training scenarios. Doing so can promote more frequent, comprehensive, and inclusive training experiences for all participants in the ATO process by providing relevant experiences for both operational-level and tactical-level participants who may be executing under a commander's intent.

Figure 2.2 provides a new framework for viewing AOC training conditions, and it illustrates, notionally, factors that AOC leadership might consider when determining their potential level of involvement in the context of four particular training scenarios. The blue boxes reflect potential constraints that affect how LVC might provide opportunities for enhancing a training experience of the ATO process. In different training scenarios, LVC technologies offer opportunities to overcome the inherent limitations. The first constraint: "Are other organizations involved?" will ultimately determine the extent of independence the AOC has over the training. The second constraint: "Will the inputs for the ATO process be provided [by the hosting organization]?" affects the degree to which the AOC might supplement training of the ATO process if the process is not adequately included in the larger exercise. The third constraint: "Will AOC participants have access to their weapon system?" affects the setting in which the ATO process will be practiced—using either the AOC weapon system or a simulator.

Four example training scenarios are summarized in the yellow boxes. The leftmost box describes a scenario in which an AOC uses LVC technology to conduct in-house training, relying on computer-generated (constructive) elements and interactions such that an individual would be able to engage in training without the participation of other AOC staff. When an individual at the AOC needs training on a particular role in the ATO process, the AOC, using LVC, could set up a live simulation for the trainee. In this scenario, that individual trainee could practice their role with constructive entities using their actual weapon system as opposed to a simulator. LVC provides scalable training opportunities that can allow training of individuals alone as well as with other individuals or even whole divisions.

Figure 2.2. Notional Framework of Potential for LVC in Different Training Settings

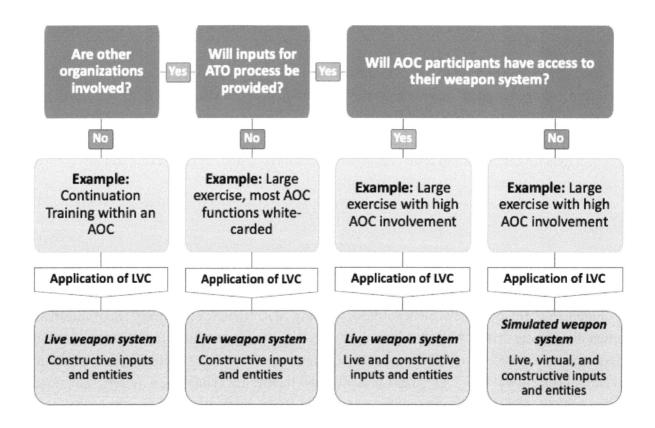

AOCs participate in larger exercises involving multiple organizations outside the AOC. Depending on the objectives of the exercise, an AOC may not be able to engage all their divisions fully, and a common practice in such cases is for some AOC functions to be white-carded. Consequently, many exercises use scripted scenarios to test flight crew operations, which neither test nor contribute to the training of AOC personnel. When white-carding occurs, it creates a training gap with the AOC playing a supporting role and not necessarily participating in a meaningful way. Conversely, AOC training scenarios might dramatically alter the desired learning objectives of the flying exercise. In such cases, increased use of virtual and constructive delivery can optimize training time and learning objectives by separating significant portions of training in a vignette delivery. A scenario in which the AOC is participating in an exercise with other organizations, but those organizations are not providing data to the AOC or utilizing AOC outputs, provides an opportunity for LVC. If the AOC is not an active participant, LVC could be used to provide a supplemental training experience. The AOC could incorporate aspects of the larger exercise, to the extent possible, while using constructive elements to fill in the gaps and run a live simulation in parallel.

When AOCs are an active participant in a multiorganization exercise, LVC can still be used to supplement specific aspects of the ATO process that may not be fully developed in the larger exercise. The two scenarios on the right-hand side of Figure 2.2 both assume that the AOC is playing a fairly involved role in a larger multidomain exercise. The primary difference between these two is that the rightmost scenario is one in which the AOC participants will not have access to their actual weapon system whereas in the second scenario from the right, they will. LVC technology can be similarly helpful in both scenarios because it can augment what would otherwise be "training support" deficiencies in the live joint training event. In both scenarios LVC offers added flexibility for AOCs to customize their training experience and ensure that no AOC staff or divisions are being overlooked.

Beyond larger exercises, this framework is scalable to more-isolated live flight training exercises. For example, given the availability of infrastructure and resources, AOC training and the ATO process could be combined with live flight training missions as part of CT. Combining training exercises in this way in different training scenarios provides an opportunity to enhance the realism and motivate the trainees through the inherent accountability that comes from participating in a combined exercise.

Conclusion

Any discussion of proper training approaches and capabilities must first consider the underlying training needs. Thus, as reference for analysis of training processes discussed in Chapter 3 and training capabilities discussed in Chapter 4, we have outlined anticipated training needs for JADC2 and the motivation for JADC2 in this chapter. We derived plausible emerging operational and training requirements from literature on how the conduct of warfare may change in the future, particularly against near-peer threats, with a focus on multidomain C2. This work was based on Air Force doctrine and existing C2 instructional programs and an extensive set of interviews with DAF and other DoD officials involved in JADC2, C2 training, and modeling and simulation. In addition to discussing how training requirements might depend on different features of JADC2, we explored how the training requirements process might drive JADC2 training implementation with some modifications. We identified specific potential uses for LVC technologies in the ATO cycle, which constitutes a primary function, and thus a primary training need within AOCs.

In general, JADC2 will enable the USAF to move from decision to action more quickly than its adversaries, and this will require faster C2 with improved interoperability (with the USAF and across the services). This in turn will require improved joint coordination, communication, and operations, all of which have been a long-standing challenge for DoD. Consequently, training to perform in such an environment will become even more important.

Findings from this analysis take the form of training needs and requirements that provide a baseline for analyses in Chapters 3 and 4. These requirements are summarized and categorized here. Employing JADC2 for its desired intent will require the following capabilities, which in turn will require appropriate training:

- the ability to **distribute and decentralize C2**, especially in the case when one or more nodes are disabled
- resources for **resilient, local C2** in the face of adversaries' ability to contest and degrade the information and communication environments
- **dynamic tasking** that is responsive to rapidly changing tactical and operational scenarios
- **the ability to sift through, fuse, and analyze data**, filtering out noise and providing the relevant information to the right decisionmaker
- the ability to conduct **C2 at a faster pace**
- the ability to form a **multidomain COP**.

Training requirements with direct implications for AOCs are as follows:

- **AOCs will likely need training capabilities that can simulate effects from other domains.** Space and cyber effects in particular pose difficulties for simulation.

  - AOCs will likely require familiarization with other domains' C2 processes and effects. More broadly, they will require a shared understanding of joint force capabilities and limitations.

- **AOCs will require operationally complex training environments in which to train for JADC2.** This will require new simulation capabilities and a move away from the frequent white-carding of such events as communications degradation. Modeling such effects remains difficult in many instances. For example, the effects of cyberattacks are not well modeled despite the need for C2 operators to detect their effects, counter adversary actions, and mitigate the effects of friendly actions.[100]
- **AOC may require new training capabilities to train alongside other AOCs and across AORs.** For example, this might look like populating the COP in one AOC with assets controlled by another AOC for purposes of deconfliction. Depending on the direction that DoD and the DAF take on alternative C2 constructs, AOCs may require new training capabilities to exercise the horizontal or vertical handoff and receipt of C2 authorities.
- JADC2 will leverage **automated decision tools (AI/ML)**, which **will require familiarization, trust, simulation capabilities, and adequate training data**.

Additional key findings are as follows:

- Due to the inherently joint nature of JADC2, **alignment among the services will be critical**. The services may not be on the right path to developing interoperable JADC2 capabilities,[101] and they lack a common understanding of what JADC2 is and how service efforts are advancing its vision.

---

[100] DAF official, interview with authors, August 6, 2021. For information on using LVC for training cyber effects, see Jennifer McCardle, "Victory over and Across Domains," Center for Strategic and Budgetary Assessments, January 25, 2019.

[101] Todd Harrison, "Battle Networks and the Future Force," Center for Strategic and International Studies, August 5, 2021.

- **The task lists as currently used are not well set up to enable training for JADC2**, and they may not help the DAF identify training requirements and develop training capabilities once JADC2 is in place. See Appendix C for details.

Chapter 3. AOC Training Processes

In this chapter, we examine the current training of Air Force AOC personnel in greater detail as the basis for understanding the potential impact of JADC2 on AOC training as well as the use of LVC tools. We primarily address three related questions. First, how does the Air Force train AOC personnel? Second, how consistent are training processes across AOCs and major commands (MAJCOMs)? And third, to what extent is centralized coordination balanced with decentralized training needs across the diverse set of regional and global AOCs?

We assess bases of standardization across the three phases of AOC training: IQT, mission qualification training (MQT), and CT. Although the focus of this study is CT, it was important to view training for JADC2 holistically and consider CT in context. Despite a degree of standardization and centralization, there is significant variation in the content, modality, and frequency of CT across AOCs. Accordingly, we examine the sources and rationale of this variation with particular emphasis on the role of external exercises. Beyond looking at current training, we also consider how the future evolution of AOC structures and processes in response to JADC2 could affect AOC training. Here, we consider the potential impact of the physical distribution of AOC functions as well as the adoption of cloud-based C2 applications at the AOC.

AOC Training and Key Roles

AOC training occurs in three phases with the overall purpose of building and maintaining combat-mission-ready (CMR) AOC crewmembers to support CCMD requirements for the operational C2 of air, space, and cyber forces. The first phase is IQT. Air Force personnel assigned to an AOC come from a wide variety of Air Force career fields with diverse Air Force Specialty Codes and varying degrees of operational experience. The intent of IQT is to provide a baseline understanding of the AOC mission and AOC processes; most AOC personnel attend IQT at a centralized formal training unit (FTU). After completion of IQT and arrival at the AOC, a new AOC crewmember starts a locally managed MQT program. During MQT, the crewmember learns about the specific mission and processes of their assigned AOC and gets hands-on experience with individual crew position duties before being officially designated CMR. After completing MQT and over the course of an AOC assignment, the crewmember receives CT to build proficiency and maintain CMR status. CT generally consists of a mix of locally conducted academics, internal AOC exercises, and external exercises. In some cases, real-world operations substitute for dedicated training events.

Many AOCs fall under a MAJCOM other than Air Combat Command (ACC), but ACC serves as the office of primary responsibility (OPR), or lead command, for the AOC weapon system and thus provides general direction and management of AOC training. Two organizations in ACC play lead roles in this regard. First, the ACC Command and Control, Intelligence, Surveillance, and Reconnaissance Operations Division (ACC/A3C) serves in both an external oversight and intermediary capacity, providing training direction down the chain to individual AOCs and training recommendations up the chain to ACC leadership. Specifically, ACC/A3C is tasked to do the following:[102]

- update *Air Force Instruction 13-1AOC Manual*, Volume 1, which establishes formal written guidance for AOC training programs
- review and provide ACC with approval recommendation for AOC IQT and any advanced AOC courseware content, training tasks, and syllabi
- coordinate with MAJCOMs and other services for class quotas to the AOC FTU
- oversee development and coordination of standardized master MQT training task lists
- establish general CT requirements for geographic AOCs (global AOCs receive CT requirements from their parent MAJCOMs)
- coordinate external training exercises with AOCs.

The second key organization under ACC is the 505th CCW. Whereas the role of ACC/A3C is primarily one of oversight and direction, the 505th CCW operates the FTU through the 505th TRS. In this capacity, the 505th CCW is tasked with the following:

- develop, maintain, and update IQT syllabi and academic lessons (submitted to ACC/A3C for approval)
- provide a semiannual report to ACC covering graduation results for each FTU course
- support AOCs in the development of in-unit IQT programs when attendance at the AOC FTU is not possible, including providing online courses, lesson plans, and test materials.

Through its subordinate 705th TRS, the 505 CCW also manages the 13O IQT program, and many of the graduates of this program move on to key roles in an AOC.[103] Furthermore, through the 505th Combat Training Squadron (CTS), the 505th CCW oversees Exercise BLUE FLAG, which focuses on operational C2 and provides valuable training for AOC personnel. Figure 3.1 illustrates the relevant organizational relationships.

---

[102] Department of the Air Force Manual 13-1AOC, Volume 1, *Ground Environment Training Air Operations Center (AOC)*, Department of the Air Force, July 29, 2019.

[103] Since this writing, the 13O career field has been discontinued. The intent of discontinuing the career field was to incorporate the skill set more widely into Air Force–wide developmental education. However, original plans for this career field still speak to the perceived need to develop multidomain C2 expertise. "Air Force to Phase Out 13O Career Field, Strengthen All Airmen Joint Capabilities," U.S. Air Force, February 17, 2022.

Figure 3.1. Significant Organizations Under Air Combat Command for AOC Training

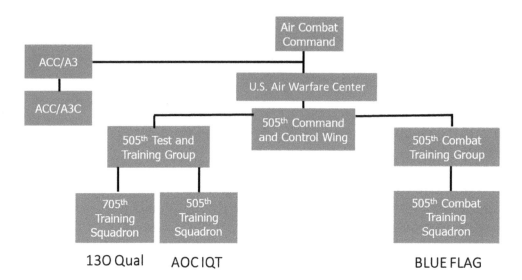

NOTE: A3 = Directorate of Air and Space Operations; Qual = Qualification.

At the AOC level, the AOC commander has significant leeway on how to apply ACC, parent MAJCOM, and other Air Force guidance when developing unit-specific MQT and CT programs.[104] Typically, the AOC commander assigns a small number of subordinates to a unit training office led by a unit training manager. Within the framework of external requirements, the unit training office builds an annual unit training plan for approval by the commander and then monitors progress over the course of the year.

Initial Qualification Training

Per Department of the Air Force Manual 13-1AOC, Volume 1, the purpose of AOC IQT is to provide foundational knowledge, skills, and context for follow-on AOC training. It does not provide in-depth positional or theater-specific training but instead teaches basic skills and establishes a common understanding of AOC processes.[105]

The 505th TRS conducts six iterations of the AOC IQT course at the FTU annually, awarding basic AOC qualification status to approximately 1,500 graduates per year. The course is typically taught in 19 training days over a four-week period, with the curriculum divided into three phases. The first phase is a relatively brief three-day block focused on C2 fundamentals with an emphasis on the structure and basic processes of the AOC, command relationships, and how the AOC integrates with joint forces as well as space and cyber enablers. For the second phase, which covers the bulk of the overall course, students break up into smaller groups based on their anticipated job at an AOC, with separate curricula for those assigned to strategy, plans,

---

[104] DAF official, interview with authors, May 13, 2021.

[105] Department of the Air Force Manual 13-1AOC, Volume 1, 2019.

operations, ISR, air mobility, airspace, and personnel recovery roles. This tailored training emphasizes how specific positions contribute to the joint targeting cycle with instruction on how to develop and execute an ATO. For the final two days, students come back together for an exercise that walks through the ATO process in a simulated combat environment. Apart from the final exercise, most of the IQT at the FTU is conducted via standard classroom format using Microsoft PowerPoint presentations. For the exercise, the 505th TRS facility includes a mock AOC floor equipped with the same Theater Battle Management Core System (TBMCS) suite of computer applications currently employed by most AOCs.

As noted above, the bulk of Air Force personnel assigned to an AOC attend centralized IQT at the FTU prior to arrival at their specific AOC location. Others are unable to attend IQT at the FTU or are not required to attend IQT at the FTU. Those in the former category are generally unable to attend because of a lack of open slots at the FTU and/or timing constraints. For these individuals, the AOC commander at their assigned AOC is responsible for providing in-unit IQT using the FTU syllabus and training materials to the maximum extent possible. A small number of AOCs have their own dedicated IQT programs, and thus few personnel assigned to these AOCs are required to attend IQT at the FTU. The 618th AOC, in particular, relies on the 435th TRS co-located at Scott Air Force Base (AFB) for providing IQT to inbound 618th AOC personnel.[106] The 616th AOC currently sends most of its inbound personnel to a generalized cyber skills course for IQT but has determined the need for more-tailored AOC training. As of 2021, the 616th AOC is working with ACC to develop a new, localized IQT course that better meets 616th AOC needs.[107] Then there are personnel who are exempt from either dedicated or in-house IQT based on attendance at an in-lieu-of (ILO) training course. Such courses include the Air Force Advanced Study of Air Mobility course for AOC personnel going to Air Mobility Division positions, the Air Force School of Advanced Air and Space Studies for those going to Strategy Division positions, and the Combined/Joint Senior Service Course for inbound division chiefs. This is not to say that all personnel going to these divisions attend ILO courses; instead, personnel attending these courses are generally exempt from an additional program. Graduates of the 13O qualification course, also managed by the 505th CCW, are generally exempt from AOC IQT as well, regardless of their anticipated role at the AOC (see Figure 3.2).

Beyond its primary training function, IQT provides an important common touchpoint for most AOC personnel before they disperse to AOCs around the globe. Accordingly, IQT represents an important lever for inculcating new concepts and new processes relevant to the AOC enterprise, including those associated with JADC2. Previously, Air Force leadership expressed concern that the FTU was not postured to meet the evolving demands of joint all-domain operations or effectively prepare students for working in a JADC2 environment because of undefined requirements, outdated course content, cumbersome teaching methods, and limited

---

[106] DAF official, interview with authors, May 7, 2021.

[107] DAF official, interview with authors, September 8, 2021.

instructor expertise.[108] As of 2021, however, the 505th TRS was in the middle of an extensive assessment and revision of the IQT program to improve in all three areas with the overall goal of creating "an immersive JADC2 training environment."[109]

Figure 3.2. AOC Training Flow

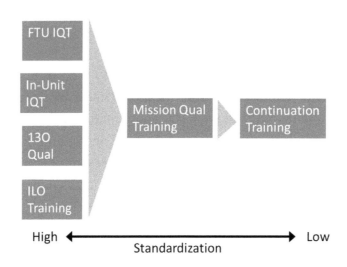

NOTE: Qual = qualification.

13O Career Field

The 13O qualification course is also an important lever for building JADC2 expertise and providing this expertise to the AOCs, and its examination can prove helpful notwithstanding the discontinuation of the career field itself. This is especially the case as the Air Force considers how to distribute the required depth of experience more widely.

As noted in Chapter 2, 13Os are trained to be C2 experts specializing in joint operations planning across domains. The career field was developed to alleviate some of the perceived capability gaps for implementation of multidomain warfare in the USAF. As of 2021, the career field was just a few years old, so the full impact is not yet known or felt. The idea behind the 13O career field is for officers to spend the first half of their careers in a different operational career field and then transition at the nine- to 12-year point to become part of a relatively small, dedicated core of multidomain C2 professionals.

Although not all graduates of the 13O qualification course go to an AOC, most do. In addition, although 13O qualification training is not necessarily tailored to an AOC assignment, the training is much more robust than the traditional AOC IQT course with a more extensive

---

[108] Department of the Air Force, "505th Training Squadron Immersion Brief," June 26, 2020b.

[109] Department of the Air Force, "505 TTG TASKING ORDER 20-03 (505 TRS MDC2/Training Model CONOP)," January 29, 2020a.

curriculum aimed at preparing officers to conduct operational-level C2 across multiple warfighting domains. Although it is valuable to add a JADC2 focus to the AOC IQT course, the FTU is constrained by the short duration of the course as well as the need to teach at a relatively basic level due to the lack of operational experience of many of the attendees. The 13O course, in contrast, is nearly five times as long and is tailored to a training audience of captains and majors with strong operational backgrounds. AOC crewmembers coming out of the FTU with a Basic Qualification will be familiar with JADC2 as a concept. AOC crewmembers coming out of the 13O Qualification course with a new career field identifier will have more in-depth knowledge of JADC2 and be postured to share this knowledge with other AOC crewmembers. According to senior Air Force officers at one AOC, 13Os play an important mentorship role and also make a significant contribution to process improvement and training program development. Of note, "The ability of 13Os to conceptualize and think creatively about multi-domain integration is extremely useful."[110]

Although the new 13O career field offers utility for building JADC2 expertise and providing this expertise to the AOC, there are three potential limitations. First, the training pipeline is slow and the number of 13Os remains relatively few.[111] Accordingly, 13O presence at AOCs remains minimal overall and inconsistent across AOCs.[112] Second, given that the 13O career field is new, it appears some Air Force leaders do not fully understand the intent or value of the career field. This translates to a lack of support, including a hesitancy to endorse their best subordinates for transition to the new career field. And third, there is some confusion across AOCs on how best to use 13Os assigned to the AOC. This has resulted in suboptimal use in some cases, with 13Os placed in AOC jobs that do not fully capitalize on unique 13O skills and expertise.[113]

Mission Qualification Training

AOC crewmembers come out of IQT with Basic Qualified status. Once at their assigned AOCs, they accomplish MQT to become CMR. Whereas IQT is more centralized and general with its focus, MQT is the responsibility of the individual AOCs and is aimed at providing the positional and theater-specific training necessary to perform the missions of a designated AOC. Each AOC determines the best mix of methods to fulfill MQT requirements. Internal to an AOC, individual divisions often manage their own MQT programs. And, given that each AOC has a distinct mission and/or geographic focus, the content of MQT curricula necessarily varies across AOCs. Still, there is a significant degree of standardization with MQT, because ACC/A3C manages the development of MQT course materials and approves a standardized MQT task list.

---

[110] DAF official, interview with authors, September 8, 2021.

[111] The Air Force planned to graduate approximately 70 new 13Os per year, eventually filling an anticipated 500 13O billets. See Rachel S. Cohen, "Moving MDC2 from Research to Reality," *Air Force Magazine*, April 15, 2019.

[112] DAF officials, interviews with authors, February 10, 2021; May 13, 2021; and June 2, 2021.

[113] DAF official, interview with authors, February 10, 2021.

Furthermore, ACC has established that AOCs are expected to start MQT within 45 days of an individual's completion of IQT, then complete MQT within 90 days of the MQT start date. And even though AOCs have a lot of leeway in terms of methods for MQT, most tend to rely heavily on supervised on-the-job training (OJT) regardless of the distinct mission and/or geographic focus.[114]

Continuation Training

After completing MQT and receiving CMR status, AOC crewmembers begin CT with the intent of building proficiency and maintaining CMR status over the course of their AOC assignment. Per Air Force guidance, CT may consist of any combination of classroom academics, directed self-study, systems training, positional procedures training, and exercises, and ACC has established broad annual CT requirements in the categories of doctrine, theater guidance, AOC systems, the operational environment, and process and positional training. In addition, ACC has directed that each crewmember at a geographic AOC participate in at least one training exercise per year as part of CT.[115]

As noted above, most AOCs currently employ TBMCS for automated air battle planning and execution management, although the Air Force has started transitioning to the Kessel Run All Domain Operations Suite (KRADOS). A key benefit of TBMCS is its well-established training capability through the Command and Control Weapon System Part Task Trainer and other applications. This allows AOC crewmembers to accomplish process and positional training via simulation on the same systems and workstations they use for daily, real-world operations. Such training can be run internally using stand-alone systems without need for external coordination, or it can interface with other virtual and constructive models in a distributed environment and can thus be used to link the AOC to external training exercises. It is important that KRADOS, once fully implemented, incorporate a similar training capability.

Training Exercises

For most AOCs, exercises are a central element of CT. AOC training exercises fall into two broad categories. The first consists of internal exercises that an AOC plans and executes with local resources. The second consists of external exercises typically sponsored by a MAJCOM or CCMD. An AOC can participate in an external exercise as a collective unit, or the AOC can designate individual crewmembers to participate in an external exercise as augmentees. The 612th AOC at Davis-Monthan AFB, Arizona, for example, tries to send 10 to 15 percent of its personnel per year to Exercise RED FLAG at Nellis AFB, Nevada.[116]

---

[114] DAF official, interview with authors, May 13, 2021, and May 26, 2021.

[115] Department of the Air Force, Manual 13-1AOC, Volume 1, 2019.

[116] DAF official, interview with authors, May 13, 2021.

ACC has identified 22 different Air Force and CCMD exercises "with AOC participation" that fulfill CT requirements, while the 505th CCW highlights an additional eight that provide AOC training opportunities.[117] It is important to recognize that not all external exercises offer the same relevance to the AOC, even among those exercises "approved" for AOC training. The AOC primarily functions at the operational level of war. In contrast, a large percentage of external exercises emphasize tactical employment and integration. Key examples here include RED FLAG, GREEN FLAG, and EMERALD WARRIOR. The AOC can support these tactical-level exercises, and individual crewmembers may gain valuable experience in their specific positions. But in general, such exercises do not provide effective training for the AOC as an integrated unit or across divisions, and these exercises generally do not capture all aspects of the ATO cycle. Discussing the limited relevance of many exercises for AOC training, one Air Force representative noted, "The difference is operational versus tactical. It's a stark difference. We really can't mix the two; they don't mesh well at all because the tactical objectives are so focused on the individual, and the operational objectives are well above that."[118] Speaking specifically of RED FLAG, another Air Force representative explained,

> With RED FLAG, there's [an] AOC white cell we put in there. It's not an entire AOC. If you want to train entire AOC, we can't do it. We bring those folks who would do the tasking. But there is a simulated AOC [operations] floor who tasks things up to the jet or whatever. There is that piece of it at RED FLAG but it's a small subset of AOC.[119]

There are also several external Air Force and CCMD exercises designated for command post training or that otherwise emphasize higher headquarters staff processes and decisionmaking. The AOC can participate in these exercises as well, but the AOC is not the primary training audience, and exercise training objectives are not typically tailored to the AOC; AOC personnel have accordingly observed that they are constrained to a supporting role with scripted participation.[120] However, there is some variation in how well these types of exercises meet AOC training needs. The 607th AOC in Korea, for example, reports gaining valuable training from two annual large-scale command post exercises on the Korean Peninsula. An important factor for the 607th AOC in this regard is the robust local modeling and simulation capability of the Pacific Air Simulation Center (PASC)—formerly the Korea Air Simulation Center—that supports these command post exercises. The 607th AOC routinely works with the PASC for small-scale internal exercises, and for the large-scale external command post exercises, the PASC is able to link the 607th AOC to the broader simulation environment in a manner that facilitates the 607th AOC

---

[117] Department of the Air Force, Manual 13-1AOC, Volume 1, 2019; Department of the Air Force, 505th Command and Control Wing, "Air Component Training Courses and Exercises," undated.

[118] DAF official, interview with authors, December 16, 2020.

[119] DAF official, interview with authors, March 10, 2021.

[120] DAF official, interview with authors, May 7, 2021.

training as a full participant.[121] Although not as common as we suggest it should be, this coordinated training environment reflects the fourth (farthest right) scenario in Figure 2.2.

Overall, most external exercises are not optimized for operational-level AOC training. Exercise BLUE FLAG represents a key exception. BLUE FLAG, which provides "a realistic, operational level, multidomain command and control decision environment utilizing high-fidelity constructive and virtual models in a simulated environment," is tailored to holistic AOC training and is built around AOC training objectives.[122] Although BLUE FLAG started in 1976 and has always focused on operational C2 in contrast to the tactics-oriented RED FLAG, the current version of the exercise with its robust suite of modeling and simulation tools was launched in 2018. Over the past couple of years, BLUE FLAG has primarily supported the 612th and 603rd AOCs, but given high demand, the 505th CCW is working to double the number of BLUE FLAG exercises it runs per year and has expanded to working with the 601st and 613th AOCs.[123] Several AOC personnel have observed that BLUE FLAG provides the best opportunity for the AOC to train as a unit in a complex and realistic warfighting scenario, the primary complaint being that a given AOC is likely to participate in a BLUE FLAG exercise every other year at best.[124]

Not surprisingly, there is a consensus across AOCs that AOC personnel receive more-effective training from exercises that employ robust LVC capabilities that tie into the AOC's existing systems as opposed to those exercises that rely on white-card injects. Beyond its focus on the operational-level C2, this is a key reason why AOCs view BLUE FLAG as a highly valuable training opportunity. And this is also why the relationship between the AOC and a local simulation center such as the PASC is important. Apart from BLUE FLAG, the optimal scenario for the AOC is one in which the 505th CTS (LVC support to BLUE FLAG and the Joint Air Component C2 Exercise, Training, and Integration [JETI] Program exercises under the 505th CCW) augments the local simulation center, which in turn coordinates closely with the AOC simulation cell and exercise planning team. Furthermore, consideration of AOC training requirements should be incorporated as early as the annual meeting of the Exercise Coordination Working Group (ECWG), chaired by ACC on behalf of the Air Force.[125] Per ECWG participants, AOC training has generally been an afterthought at these foundational meetings which tend to focus more on tactical flying units.[126] Furthermore, as shown in Figure 3.3, the use of LVC to enhance AOC training should be factored into each stage of the exercise life cycle

---

[121] DAF official, interview with authors, August 18, 2021, and September 9, 2021.

[122] Department of the Air Force, 505th Command and Control Wing, undated.

[123] DAF official, interview with authors, August 3, 2021.

[124] DAF official, interview with authors, May 13, 2021.

[125] See Air Force Instruction 10-204, *Air Force Service Exercise Program and Support to Joint and National Exercise Program*, Department of the Air Force, April 12, 2019.

[126] DAF official, interview with authors, August 3, 2021.

from concept development through postexercise analysis. Training exercises, for which there is already a planning and execution mechanism, represent an accessible venue for leveraging LVC as JADC2 develops and training needs evolve. However, LVC is not necessarily integrated as often and as effectively as it could be.

Figure 3.3. Integration of LVC into the Air Force Exercise Life Cycle

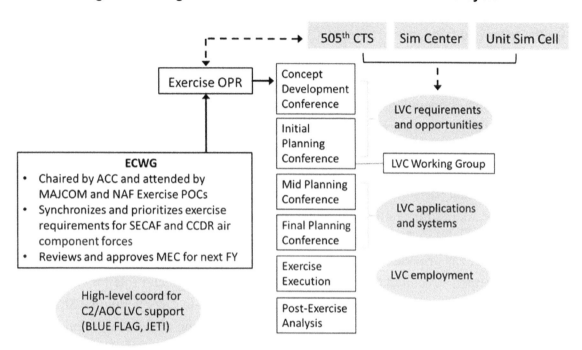

NOTE: CCDR = combatant commander; coord = coordination; FY = fiscal year; POC = point of contact; MEC = master exercise calendar; NAF = Numbered Air Force; SECAF = Secretary of the Air Force; Sim = simulation.

Variation in AOC Continuation Training

As discussed above, AOC IQT provides a centralized foundation for crewmembers across AOCs. Although not all AOC personnel go through the same IQT program, there is a high level of standardization in each program and across most programs. The 505th CCW provides curriculum support for FTU IQT, in-house IQT, 13O qualification, and even ILO programs, such as the Air Force School of Advanced Air and Space Studies and the Combined/Joint Senior Service Course.

In contrast, we see significant variation with CT across AOCs. Given the different regional and functional priorities of the different AOCs, there is necessary and expected variation in the content of training curricula. But there is also significant variation across AOCs in terms of the frequency and modality of training. The Air Force distinguishes between geographic AOCs, which support operations in a designated geographic CCMD, and global AOCs, which serve a specific functional role across geographic CCMDs. This distinction affects the administrative oversight of AOC training and is the source of some training variation, but the differences we see

41

in the frequency and modality of training across AOCs derive from other characteristics as well. Important sources of variation include the following:

- parent MAJCOM-specific training guidance
- the gap between steady-state and contingency AOC operations
- the extent of integration with joint forces across multiple warfighting domains
- manning levels and steady-state operations tempo
- internal LVC capabilities and/or dedicated exercise simulation support
- the focus and frequency of parent CCMD and MAJCOM exercises.

One of the most important sources of variation is the gap between peacetime and wartime operations, or *steady-state* and *contingency* operations. For some AOCs, the gap is minimal, even if the intensity of operations is likely to increase in the event of war. The global airlift mission of the 618th AOC, for example, looks similar across the spectrum of conflict. In contrast, the 607th AOC will function fully only in the event of a war on the Korean Peninsula. There is some correlation here with the geographic versus global categorical distinction, but there is still significant variation across AOCs of the same category. Comparing the 612th and 613th geographic AOCs, for example, the gap between peacetime and wartime operations is greater with the latter.

This distinction has important implications for AOC training. For *low-gap* AOCs, there is less need for a formal, structured CT program. Instead, there is a greater role for OJT; AOC crewmembers gain and maintain necessary proficiency via day-to-day operations. Similarly, there is less impetus for exercises and simulation aimed at training crewmembers on the mission. Going back to the 618th AOC, for example, the primary emphasis of internal exercises is on *continuity of operations*, or how to operate from a contingency facility if the main AOC facility becomes unusable for any number of reasons. These exercises are not necessarily used to train crewmembers on the mission but instead test their ability to do the mission from an alternate location. They achieve this by physically moving to an alternate location once or twice per year. In contrast, for *high-gap* AOCs, day-to-day peacetime operations do not adequately prepare crewmembers for the wartime mission. OJT is useful for teaching basic skills and processes, but there is much greater demand for a dedicated CT program emphasizing exercises and simulation. Figure 3.4 illustrates the range of this gap.

Figure 3.4. How AOCs Differ with Steady-State Versus Contingency Operations

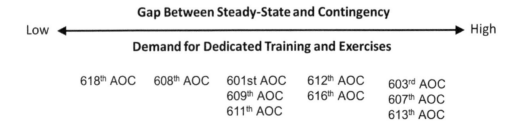

Given the importance of the decentralized and sometimes unique training needs across AOCs, we step through Figure 3.4 in detail, as follows. The 603rd, 607th, 609th, and 613th AOCs are the more-traditional warfighting AOCs; the 603rd and 613th AOCs particularly focus on potential major combat operations against a near-peer adversary. The 609th AOC is distinct in this grouping because U.S. Central Command has seen near-continuous contingency operations for the past 20 years. Of course, there could be an increase in intensity—for example, in the event of a war between the United States and Iran—but the peacetime-wartime gap with the 609th AOC is narrower than seen in comparable geographic AOCs because of the steady-state wartime context. Recent participation of the 609th AOC in external exercises has been more focused on integrated missile defense in the U.S. Central Command region as opposed to more-traditional C2 of air assets. The 612th AOC, which covers the U.S. Southern Command (SOUTHCOM) geographic CCMD, generally exhibits a lesser peacetime-wartime gap than other geographic AOCs because of the lower probability of major combat operations in the SOUTHCOM theater. With SOUTHCOM, we see a priority on providing humanitarian assistance, building partner capacity, and countering transnational criminal organizations. Accordingly, contingency scenarios in SOUTHCOM do not vary as much from steady-state operations. The 608th AOC, which is responsible for providing C2 for global strike missions, obviously has an important wartime function. However, the role of the 608th AOC is generally limited to the planning and C2 necessary to move strike assets to a given location in support of geographic CCMD requirements, and this does not change significantly across peacetime and wartime deployments. It is not surprising, then, that the 608th AOC relies primarily on OJT with very little dedicated training. The 608th AOC does participate in CCMD-level (U.S. Strategic Command) exercises such as Exercise GLOBAL THUNDER, but this is primarily in support of CCMD, not AOC, training objectives. AOC personnel with experience at both the 608th AOC and the 613th AOC have noted a sharp difference in the importance of simulation, with far more use of simulation in training at the 613th than at the 608th AOC.[127]

The gap between steady-state and contingency operations is relevant not only to AOCs as units but also to individual divisions within an AOC. For example, personnel at multiple AOCs have noted a significant difference between the ISR Division and the Combat Operations Division, with the former better able to meet its training needs through day-to-day operations in a peacetime or competition context.[128]

Another key distinction among AOCs with implications for training is the extent to which an AOC's mission requires integration across domains and across the joint force. This affects the extent to which an AOC can achieve effective training via local, internal training programs, with greater integration driving a demand for exercises with external players or at least the simulation of external players. Global AOCs, such as the 608th, 616th, and 618th, tend to be limited to a

---

[127] DAF official, interview with authors, May 13, 2021.

[128] DAF officials, interviews with authors, May 13, 2021, and April 21, 2021.

single domain. Geographic AOCs, such as the 603rd, 607th, 609th, and 613th, are more tailored to joint, all-domain operations. The 612th AOC, although less of a traditional warfighting AOC, still exhibits significant integration with joint forces across multiple domains. Personnel from high-integration AOCs have observed that one of the main constraints on effective training is difficulty in scheduling joint assets.[129] The 601st and 611th AOCs, while also in the geographic category, are predominantly focused on the air domain and have less routine coordination with ground or maritime forces. Thus, for the 601st and 611th AOCs, internal exercises and limited in-house simulation capabilities fulfill training needs to a greater extent than seen with other geographic AOCs.

Although the importance of external exercises varies across AOCs, all AOCs participate in external exercises to augment internal CT. As noted above, individual AOC crewmembers can readily participate in exercises outside their parent CCMD or MAJCOM, but AOC-level participation is generally weighted to those exercises sponsored by the parent CCMD or MAJCOM. Because of this, the frequency and emphasis of these CCMD and MAJCOM exercises have a significant impact on AOC training and on the variation in training we see across AOCs. U.S. Forces Korea, for example, a subunified command of INDOPACOM, generally runs three major military exercises per year on the Korean Peninsula. Accordingly, the 607th AOC generally participates in three external exercises per year. Apart from monthly academics, the 607th AOC's primary method of CT is conducting internal exercises on a monthly basis.[130] In contrast, the 603rd AOC typically participates in at least one significant external exercise per month given a more expansive requirement to support wing, component, North Atlantic Treaty Organization (NATO), MAJCOM, and partner nation exercises in both U.S. European Command (EUCOM) and U.S. Africa Command (AFRICOM). The 603rd AOC has the same capability as the 607th AOC to run internal exercises, but it conducts relatively fewer internal exercises because of its participation in a much greater number of external exercises.[131] Of note, this difference in number of internal and external exercises is not necessarily based on different training needs of the AOCs but is instead driven by factors external to the AOCs.

Some AOCs also have a training advantage over others based on being co-located with a regional simulation center that offers LVC tools beyond internal AOC capability with TBMCS. As noted above, the 607th AOC works routinely with the PASC located at Osan Air Base, South Korea, to enhance the AOC's internal exercises. As of 2021, the PASC has also started engaging more with the 613th AOC in Hawaii to develop a similar training relationship.[132] Historically, the U.S. Air Forces in Europe–Air Forces Africa (USAFE-AFAFRICA) Warfare Center

---

[129] DAF officials, interviews with authors, May 13, 2021, and June 1, 2021.

[130] DAF official, interview with authors, September 9, 2021.

[131] DAF official, interview with authors, May 17, 2021.

[132] DAF official, interview with authors, August 18, 2021.

(UAWC) in Germany, with its primary focus on tactical-level exercises for USAFE-AFAFRICA, EUCOM, NATO, and AFRICOM, has not provided as much direct support to the 603rd AOC as seen between the UAWC and the 607th AOC. But also as of 2021, the UAWC has opened discussions with the 603rd AOC on ways to enhance the 603rd AOC's internal training exercise program.[133]

On a related note, as of 2021, the Air Force has started the process of transitioning AOCs from TBMCS to KRADOS, but this transition is still in a very early stage and has not been uniform across AOCs. For those AOCs that have started the process, there is an additional training requirement associated with learning the new applications, not just for personnel currently at the AOC but also for those arriving from IQT, because IQT is still primarily based on TBMCS. Furthermore, some AOC personnel have expressed concern that the initial version of KRADOS lacks the organic simulation capability of TBMCS.[134] It is probable that KRADOS will eventually incorporate a similar training feature, but as of 2021, the timing of such development is unclear. The lack of organic simulation capability directly affects internal training. But it can also matter for participation in external exercises. With Exercise BLUE FLAG, for example, the 505th CCW relies on linking its own modeling and simulation capabilities to the AOC's local simulation capability. This is currently not possible to do to the same extent with KRADOS as with TBMCS.

Finally, we observe significant variation across AOC training programs simply due to such factors as manning levels and operations tempo. Multiple AOCs report being chronically understaffed; some routinely operate with less than 40 percent of designated personnel. This exacerbates the effects of an already high operations tempo and results in little time for effective training.[135] Overall, as manning levels drop, we should expect to observe a decline in the level and extent of AOC training. This applies to both internal training programs and participation in external exercises, particularly in terms of opportunities for individuals to take time away from their assigned AOC to participate in external exercises as augmentees. The 607th AOC is an interesting and somewhat unique case in this regard. The 607th AOC is a combined AOC between the USAF and the Republic of Korea Air Force (ROKAF). ROKAF personnel are responsible for many of the day-to-day functions of the AOC under armistice conditions. This helps free up USAF personnel to some extent to train for the combat environment.[136] Table 3.1 summarizes the sources and types of training variation for AOCs.

---

[133] DAF official, interview with authors, May 18, 2021.

[134] DAF officials, interviews with authors, August 3, 2021, and May 21, 2021.

[135] DAF officials, interviews with authors, June 2, 2021, and September 9, 2021.

[136] DAF official, interview with authors, September 9, 2021.

Table 3.1. Sources and Types of Variation in AOC Continuation Training

Sources of Variation	Types of Variation
Parent MAJCOM guidance	Content of training curricula
Steady-state versus contingency operations	Balance of dedicated training versus OJT
Domain focus (single versus multiple)	Dedicated training methods and use of LVC
Interaction with joint or allied partners	Frequency and scale of internal exercises
Internal or local LVC capability	Frequency and level of external exercises
Parent MAJCOM and CCMD exercises	Training with joint or allied partners
Manning level and operations tempo	Positional versus AOC-level training

How Changes to the AOC Will Affect Training

With the emergence of JADC2, the Air Force is considering potential impacts on AOC structure and processes. Although the evolution of the AOC is an important issue in its own right, our interest here pertains to any concurrent effects on AOC training. As of 2021, there was no overarching plan to alter the AOC construct. ACC has put together a team to assess the future of the AOC, but this process is still in an early stage and has not yet produced any refined recommendations. Overall, it is likely that the AOC will change incrementally as JADC2-related concepts and systems mature and as the Air Force experiments with different approaches. Per Air Force leadership, these "exploratory efforts" will inform "continually evolving AOC processes."[137]

There will also likely be a local, organic element of AOC change. Individual MAJCOMs and AOCs have significant leeway with internal AOC organization, and currently, no two AOCs look the same regardless of any effects of JADC2. In addition, it is important to recognize that, as a concept, JADC2 will not likely apply across AOCs in the same way and to the same extent. JADC2 will be important for all AOCs, but there may be more relevance for some AOCs than others given the factors that are driving the development of JADC2. As noted above, some AOCs already have missions that are more joint and more multidomain than those of other AOCs. In addition, the anticipated level and complexity of the adversary threat in a given theater matters in that the evolution of JADC2 is driven in large part by the need for resilient C2 in a highly contested environment. A further aim of JADC2 is to provide more-effective communication and coordination of joint assets across geographic regions. The impact of JADC2 on the structure and processes of a given AOC will thus hinge to some extent on the domain focus of the AOC, the level of adversary threat, and the requirement to operate across geographic regions. Table 3.2 categorizes the *relative* weight of each of these factors across geographic and global AOCs. We assess that, for any given AOC, a higher level of transregional and multidomain activity associated with the mission along with greater likelihood of operating in a

---

[137] DAF official, interview with authors, May 21, 2021.

highly contested environment equates to more relevance of JADC2 to the AOC's operations. With the 607th AOC at Osan Air Base, for example, we assess a relatively low level of transregional activity given its primary focus on the Korean Peninsula, a relatively high level of multidomain operations, and a relatively moderate threat level in terms of a contested environment (particularly compared with what the United States might face in a Taiwan scenario versus China). We accordingly rate the impact of JADC2 as medium. In general, assuming that the evolution of JADC2 will drive at least some corresponding change to AOC structures and processes, we expect to see more-significant changes in those AOCs most affected by JADC2. This suggests that the impetus for change is likely to be highest with the 603rd and the 613th, which service INDOPACOM, EUCOM, and AFRICOM. Other AOCs in other commands will certainly benefit from JADC2 once implemented, but the need to alter their existing C2 structures is less pressing.

Table 3.2. Comparative Impact of JADC2 on AOCs

AOC	Transregional Activity	Multidomain Operations	Threat Level	Impact of JADC2
601	Low	Medium	Low	Low
603	Medium	High	High	High
607	Low	High	Medium	Medium
608	High	Medium	Medium	Medium-High
609	Low	High	Medium	Medium
611	Low	Medium	Low	Low
612	Low	High	Low	Low-Medium
613	Medium	High	High	High
616	High	Low	Low	Low-Medium
618	High	Low	Low	Low-Medium

Potential Changes to AOC Divisional Structure

JADC2 simultaneously incentivizes both the centralization and distribution of C2, and various Air Force conceptions of the future AOC diverge along this spectrum. As noted in Chapter 2, effective JADC2 requires the ability to distribute and decentralize C2 in the face of adversaries' ability to contest and degrade the information and communication environments. At the same time, JADC2 hinges on the ability to form a multidomain COP and to synchronize operational effects seamlessly across domains and geographic boundaries, which is difficult to do without some degree of centralized coordination and control.

Some Air Force leaders, noting the growing irrelevance of geographical boundaries, envision the consolidation of regional AOCs into a global operations center with a global JFACC. Others, focused on the need for operational resiliency and an increasing capability to rapidly disseminate information, propose breaking apart the AOC as we know it into smaller, more tailorable, and more agile pieces.[138] Either approach is a divergence from the status quo with implications for training. As described by Carpenter in his application of the concept of mission command to USAF C2, development of trust is essential, and tactical commanders will need to understand that operational and higher-level commanders trust them to accept prudent risk and execute actions under conditions when full communication is impossible.[139] This necessitates time to learn—for both operational and higher commanders as well as tactical—to use mission command to convey intent and trust tactical-level commanders to execute it to the best of their ability. More recently, discussion of the evolution of mission command highlighted the utility of exercises to help develop practical methods and systems of execution.[140]

Despite this uncertainty and the myriad of future AOC possibilities, there are two relatively consistent themes that emerge from the ongoing debate about the future of the AOC. The first is a distribution of at least some of the AOC functions even if control remains centralized.[141] The second is greater connectivity and collaboration among the AOC, tactical elements, and key enablers via a resilient, cloud-based network. As the *Air Force Future Operating Concept* notes, "The permanent, infrastructure-heavy theater AOCs . . . have evolved into MDOCs that can quickly be repositioned, reconfigured, and augmented."[142] Furthermore, "[m]any of the mission specific functions of AOCs have merged or moved to geographically dispersed reach-back cells with globally networked capabilities." The shift from TBMCS to KRADOS at the AOC is specifically designed around the idea of a distributed, cloud-based ATO process.[143] And, in 2018, the Air Force developed and assessed the virtual MDOC alternative as part of a Doolittle wargaming event aimed at exploring multidomain warfighting concepts.[144] This version of the virtual MDOC combined a cloud-based virtual multidomain operations environment and AI tools to accelerate the operational planning and assessment process while synchronizing inputs and feedback from a diverse set of stakeholders beyond the traditional AOC.

Figure 3.5 illustrates the conventional geographic (regional) AOC structure with five main divisions, supported by the global (functional) AOC. Figure 3.6 illustrates a potential, and notional, way to distribute some of the AOC capability to an MDOC Forward (MDOC-F) as described in the *Air Force Future Operating Concept*. In this case, the AOC still exists but

---

[138] See Priebe et al., 2020.

[139] Trent R. Carpenter, "Command and Control of Joint Air Operations Through Mission Command," *Air & Space Power Journal*, Summer 2016.

[140] Mulgund, 2021.

[141] DAF official, interview with authors, January 21, 2021.

[142] U.S. Air Force, 2015, p. 14.

[143] For Air Force statements on this topic, see Brian W. Everstine, "AFCENT Can Now Generate Air Tasking Orders in the Cloud," *Air Force Magazine*, May 14, 2021.

[144] Air Force Lessons Learned, 2019. Also see Lingel et al., 2020.

serves in more of a reach-back role to support the MDOC-F. Finally, Figure 3.7 depicts a diverse set of organizations linked through a cloud-based network to feed into the operational planning and execution cycle traditionally managed internal to the AOC, along the lines of the virtual multidomain operations environment concept presented at the 2018 Doolittle wargaming event. Overall, it is important to recognize that, while distinct, the emergent concepts of distributed AOC capabilities and cloud-based C2 processes are neither mutually exclusive nor necessarily linked. The shift to a cloud-based operational C2 application could occur in conjunction with or apart from any physical distribution of the AOC.

Figure 3.5. Conventional AOC Divisional Structure

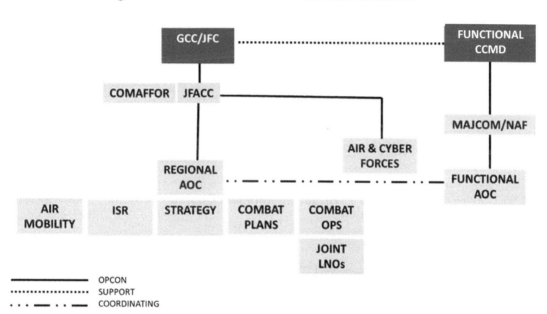

NOTE: COMAFFOR = commander, Air Force forces; GCC = geographic combatant commander; JFC = joint force commander; LNO = liaison officer; OPCON = operational control; OPS = operations.

Figure 3.6. AOC Capabilities Distributed Forward

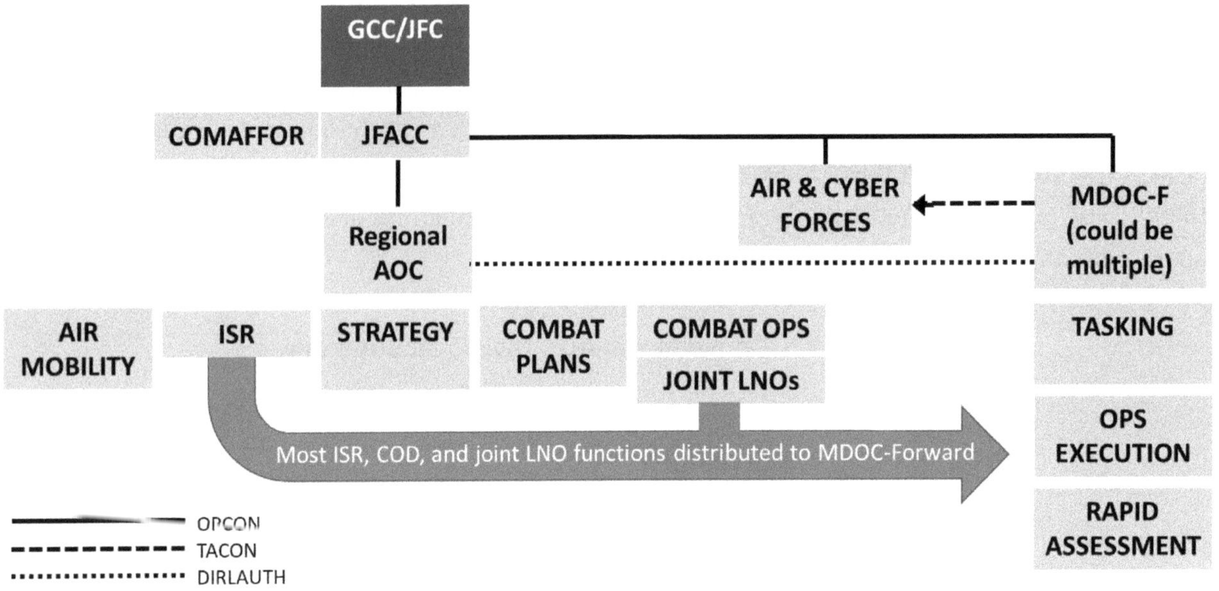

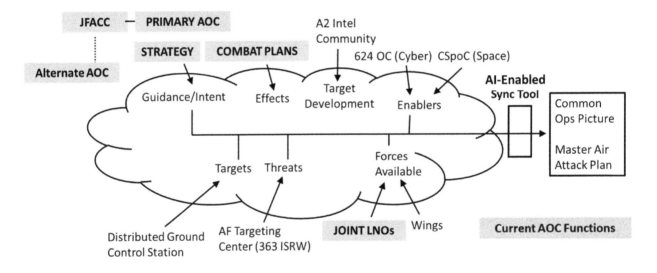

NOTE: COD = Combat Operations Division; DIRLAUTH = direct liaison authorized relationship; TACON = tactical control.

Figure 3.7. Virtual Multidomain Operations Center

NOTE: A2 = intelligence directorate; CSpoC = Combined Space Operations Center; ISRW = ISR Wing; OC = operations center.

Training Implications and the Role of LVC

This broad vision of future AOC structures and processes has important training implications and points to an even more pronounced role for LVC. To start, with the established AOC, there are already significant challenges with training the AOC *as an integrated unit* despite most AOC personnel working in the same building. Breaking up the AOC and its various functions and processes into smaller, distributed units that rely on a diverse network of reach-back cells would change the meaning of "internal" AOC training and drive an increased demand for distributed training methods. Furthermore, given the coordination and scheduling challenges associated with bringing dispersed units and functions together for routine training, there will likely be more need for virtual and constructive tools to provide a training environment that captures the interaction of multiple smaller C2 nodes. At the same time, smaller, distributed operational C2 nodes may have less organic or local LVC training capability than the current infrastructure-heavy AOC. There will accordingly be more impetus for seamless, routine access to distributed training opportunities, ideally that provide training of the quality and fidelity of a BLUE FLAG exercise without the need for the AOC to schedule and coordinate many months in advance.

The incorporation of cloud-based operational C2 processes, including ATO production and execution, along with physical distribution would further push the AOC training paradigm toward a need for LVC. As noted in the preceding chapter, even without a fundamental change in AOC structure, JADC2 will drive a requirement for more-complex training environments with new modeling and simulation capabilities, including new training capabilities to exercise the horizontal or vertical handoff and receipt of C2 authorities. With this virtual MDOC concept, C2 authorities are more fluid, and the operational planning and assessment process is less linear. Such changes would only increase the need for new LVC capabilities to effectively train AOC personnel for this environment. Even if an assumption is made that the changes described here will not require a need for LVC training for the purposes of the AOCs themselves, the AOC serves as a node of the larger C2 network incorporating tactical assets that will use the full variety of LVC capabilities. Moreover, as noted earlier, tactical commanders will need to understand that operational and higher-level commanders trust them to accept prudent risk and execute actions under conditions when full communication is impossible, and development of that trust will require practice. Accordingly, the AOC must be able to link to those LVC technologies. This need will only be more intense over time.

Conclusion

In this chapter, we examined the current training of Air Force AOC personnel as the basis for understanding the use of LVC tools as well as the potential impact of JADC2 on AOC training. We addressed three related questions. First, how does the Air Force train AOC personnel? Second, how consistent are training processes across AOCs and MAJCOMs? And third, to what extent is centralized coordination balanced with decentralized training needs across the diverse set of regional and global AOCs?

In answering these questions, we provided a review of AOC-related curricula for IQT, MQT, and CT, identifying gaps and opportunities for improvement. As part of our assessment of CT, we reviewed the training-exercise planning process and how LVC should factor in this process most effectively. We also highlighted sources of variation in training among different classes of AOCs. Finally, we looked at the current and potential structure of AOCs, how structure may affect training, and how it may facilitate the use of LVC.

It was evident from our analysis that no AOC trains the same way. When it comes to CT in particular, we observed significant variation in training across AOCs. This includes variation in the extent to which AOCs employ LVC tools to enhance their training programs. Some of this variation reflects a healthy balance between centralized coordination and decentralized training needs and stems from the fact that AOCs have different missions, structures, operational processes, and external stakeholders. However, different AOCs also face distinct training challenges—including personnel shortfalls, high operations tempo, limited external exercise opportunities, and lack of local LVC training capability—that drive training variation across AOCs in a less positive sense. The emergence of JADC2 will likely provide impetus to make changes to AOC structures and processes, but this will affect some AOCs more than others; and the more significant the evolution of AOC structures and processes in response to JADC2, the greater the potential need for LVC to effectively train AOC personnel.

A pervasive challenge with training curricula—and training in general across DoD—is the balance between centralized coordination to maximize efficiency and decentralized training needs that reflect unique mission sets and challenges. As the lead command for the AOC weapon system, ACC provides some degree of centralized oversight and coordination of AOC CT. Beyond establishing basic annual CT requirements, ACC plays a key role in scheduling AOC participation in external exercises as chair of the Air Force's ECWG. In addition, as the lead MAJCOM for BLUE FLAG, ACC has a particularly important role in determining AOC participation in what many AOC personnel consider the most valuable external training exercise. However, there is a great deal of decentralization as well, and every AOC is different in terms of the content, modality, and extent of CT. Much of this variation reflects decentralized training needs based on distinct geographical and functional roles as well as the preferences of individual AOC commanders, who are given a lot of leeway in shaping their AOC training programs. Furthermore, some AOCs have more demand for LVC training capabilities than other AOCs. Variation in training is also driven by different opportunities and limitations in a way that is not necessarily reflective of decentralized training needs. Factors such as manning shortfalls and the availability of a local simulation center dedicated to exercise support fall in this latter category.

Beyond these general observations, our assessment of current AOC training yielded several more-specific findings, summarized as follows:

- Of the three phases of AOC training, **IQT has the greatest degree of standardization and provides an important touchpoint for introducing JADC2 concepts into AOC processes**. The Air Force is revising the AOC FTU curriculum to provide an immersive JADC2 training environment. But given the limited duration and scope of IQT, any coverage of JADC2 will likely be relatively basic.

- **The 13O training pipeline, as an alternative to AOC IQT for a select group of airmen, is a potentially valuable lever** for building JADC2 expertise and providing this expertise to the AOCs. Although it is still too early to make an effective assessment, this potential is currently limited by the low number of available 13O personnel and the lack of understanding of how to employ them at the AOCs most effectively. The 13O training pipeline is not meant to fully replace AOC IQT and will likely never match IQT for throughput. Instead, the 13O training pipeline can serve as a valuable source of core expertise in JADC2 for the AOC, and its training processes can still be informative as the Air Force moves to discontinue the career field.

- **There is significant variation in CT across AOCs.** Some of this variation reflects a purposeful balance between centralized coordination and decentralized training needs; however, this variation also stems from relative gaps in resources and training opportunities from one AOC to the next. For some AOCs, personnel gain necessary proficiency via day-to-day operations, and thus there is little need for dedicated training, particularly dedicated training that employs LVC capabilities. For others, a robust dedicated training program enabled by LVC is critical to prepare for the wartime mission.

- **For many AOCs, organic training resources and LVC capabilities are not adequate to train the AOC holistically as a unit** across the scope of potential contingency scenarios. All AOCs have some internal simulation capability that is useful for partial task or procedural training, but this capability does not meet all training requirements.

- **All AOCs rely on external exercises to some extent to supplement internal CT, but not all external exercises, even those that the Air Force identified for AOC training opportunities, provide the AOC with effective training for planning and executing the entire ATO cycle.** Most external exercises emphasize either higher headquarters decisionmaking or tactical-level employment. The AOC can participate in these exercises but often does so in a supporting role and is not the primary training audience.

- **BLUE FLAG exercises are uniquely tailored to AOC training needs.** These exercises are particularly valuable given their emphasis on operational C2. However, given limited resources, the 505th CCW can typically incorporate a given AOC into a BLUE FLAG only once every other year. AOCs would benefit from training at the level of a BLUE FLAG on a more routine basis.

- **Local simulation centers, dedicated to exercise support and the relationship among the AOC and the centers, can help fill the gap between the AOC's limited organic LVC capabilities and the periodic large-scale external exercises.** A model in this regard is the working relationship between the 607th AOC and the PASC at Osan Air Base, Korea. The PASC provides LVC support to the 607th AOC for monthly internal training events and helps integrate the 607th AOC into U.S. Forces Korea's large-scale command post exercises.

- **The development of JADC2 will drive changes in AOC structures and/or processes, and the demand for LVC training capability will likely expand as the AOC evolves in response to JADC2.** The impact of JADC2 will not be the same across all AOCs, but for some, JADC2 will drive significant changes to AOC structures and processes. In particular, we expect to see greater distribution of AOC functions and the incorporation of a cloud-based architecture that is less reliant on fixed infrastructure to manage key AOC processes. Each of these evolutions will alter the AOC training paradigm in a way that increases the need for LVC training capabilities.

Chapter 4. Capabilities to Support JADC2 Training: State of the Art

Using the training needs and processes presented in Chapter 2 and Chapter 3 respectively, in this chapter, we assess multiple levels of LVC-related capabilities with respect to their ability to respond to appropriate needs in the context of current AOC training processes. The overarching questions we respond to in this chapter are as follows:

- What are the current technical capabilities and challenges for JADC2 training?
- What are the current technical capabilities and challenges for LVC, relevant to JADC2 training?

In this chapter, we map LVC-related underlying technologies, developing systems, and existing systems to aspects of JADC2 training. Although previous sections have an AOC focus, it is important to note that JADC2 includes other nodes, and some of the LVC technologies discussed are primarily relevant to other nodes comprising the JADC2 concept.

As a baseline for evaluating capabilities that are currently available or under development, we first assess the perceived value of LVC technology in the DAF and DoD, based on published training and technology road maps. Presumably, the development and use of LVC technology should align with a perceived need.

After a brief discussion of underlying LVC technologies, we itemize and assess operational systems at AOCs, noting where the LVC technologies may be applied. With this assessment of technology and (potential) training systems, we then review LVC-related DoD R&D programs (including Block 20 weapon systems and planned ABMS lines of effort) that might respond to any gaps in LVC technology and/or systems relevant to JADC2 training.

Often, reviews of training capabilities and software tend to focus on actual training systems and neglect the necessary underlying IT architecture necessary to integrate such systems. Thus, given a review of tools, capabilities, and programs, the major technological underpinnings comprising a technical architecture for JADC2 is then articulated from an IT perspective. This facilitates a common understanding of the role of IT in all-domain operations. A consequent chart highlights the commonality of challenges that all the services and partnering nations face as each implements its contribution to all-domain operations.

With a thorough review of LVC technologies, including IT systems, and how these technologies can support AOC systems and JADC2 in general, we then turn to actual distributed training systems. A key aspect of LVC and virtual training in general, especially when considering C2, is the availability of distributed training and the systems that support it. Thus, existing and in-development distributed training systems are discussed for their contribution to

JADC2 training. Finally, the complexities of incorporating LVC training for space and cyber domains are reviewed.

LVC and Its Perceived Value

As a starting point for assessing which capabilities are *currently* available or under development, we review plans for future developments as an indication of the perceived value of LVC in the DAF and across DoD more broadly. The perceived value of LVC (and its components) and even the meaning of LVC can vary across documents and organizations. Thus, in assessing whether current capabilities respond to JADC2 training needs, it is important first to understand the perceived benefits of LVC and plans for future R&D from the perspective of DoD and the DAF. Table 4.1 summarizes the perceived benefits of LVC technology across DoD and the DAF. The strategic documents referenced were published between 2016 and 2021 by the DAF or DoD. Note that the JADC2 concept was not formally initiated until 2020, and the most recent National Defense Strategy was not published until 2018, which has shifted the focus of DoD from counterinsurgency operations to peer adversaries.

Both DoD and the DAF recognize that LVC technology is critical for training the future force to fight wars of the future. There are similarities and differences between the DAF's perceived benefits of LVC technology and DoD's perceived benefits of LVC technology. In strategic level documentation (Headquarters Air Force [HAF], Air Education and Training Command, ACC, and DoD documents), DoD and the DAF have identified benefits of LVC technology for training future soldiers, seamen, airmen, guardians, and marines. DoD and the DAF have identified training benefits that LVC technology provide, such as rapidly adaptable training, integration of stakeholders for training, overcoming live training limitations, enhanced operational performance, and operational realism. For example, both DoD and the DAF highlight the pace at which LVC technology can adapt to evolving threats as a key benefit to training with LVC technology. Below, we will highlight the advantages of LVC technology: those that the DAF and DoD recognize and the differences between them.

One key difference is that the DAF has identified several additional areas in which LVC technology would be beneficial. Specifically, the DAF claims that LVC technology could require less manning, be cost-effective, and overcome regulation limitations. The DAF emphasizes the need for reduced manning support as a key area in which constructive elements can supplement training (instead of live elements) and provide value. DoD doctrine, however, does not emphasize manning as a key benefit of LVC technology.

Table 4.1. Perceived Benefits of LVC Technology in DoD and DAF Strategic Documents

Capability	Perceived Benefit of LVC Technology	DoD	DAF
Less manning resources	Reduce manning resources (supplement with constructive and/or virtual personnel or reduce travel time because training can take place through distributed means at home station) (Department of the Air Force, 2017).		X
	Create a faster training pipeline for pilots (addresses pilot shortage) (Barrett and Goldfein, 2020).		X
Cost-effectiveness	Enhance cost-effectiveness of training (Department of the Air Force, 2017).		X
Rapidly adaptable	Rapidly field updates to modernize for test and/or training and keep up with pace of changing peer threats (e.g., emulate threats instead of creating or acquiring new systems); faster-than-live environments are supported (Air Combat Command, 2020b; U.S. Department of Defense, 2020).	X	X
Integration of stakeholders	Enable and enhance joint force and DoD counterparts training (DoD Instruction 5000.02, 2020; Department of the Air Force, forthcoming; Department of the Air Force, 2017).	X	X
	Increase quantity of stakeholders (up to the thousands) (Department of the Air Force, forthcoming).		X
	Support geographically separated stakeholders (across global stage) (Department of the Air Force, forthcoming). Enhance joint training relationships (Department of the Air Force, forthcoming).		X
Overcomes regulation limitations	Enable training in simulated environments, which is not achievable in live environments due to regulations (i.e., jamming and unmanned aerial system [UAS] limitations of flight) (Department of the Air Force, 2016).		X
Overcomes live training limitations	Create multiple configurable scenarios for repeatable training (Department of the Air Force, 2016).		X
	Conduct training that would be unsafe in a live environment (Department of the Air Force, 2016).		X
	Conduct distributed training (Department of the Air Force, forthcoming; Department of the Air Force, 2016).		X
	Train with systems that can be used only once (Department of the Air Force, 2016).		X
	Connect disparate training systems in a common environment (data processing across disparate systems into common understanding) (Department of the Air Force, forthcoming).		X
	Create a classified environment (Department of the Air Force, forthcoming; U.S. Department of Defense, 2020; Department of the Air Force, 2017).	X	X

Capability	Perceived Benefit of LVC Technology	DoD	DAF
Enhances operational performance	Develop new tactics, techniques, and procedures (TTP) (Department of the Air Force, forthcoming; Department of Defense, 2020; Department of the Air Force, 2017; Department of the Air Force, 2016).	X	X
	Achieve realistic threat density (Department of the Air Force, 2017).	X	
	Increase proficiency of operator (Department of the Air Force, forthcoming; Department of Defense, 2020; Air Combat Command, 2020b). Enhance agile and robust decisionmaking under uncertainty (Department of the Air Force, 2017).	X	X X
Enhances operational realism	Train across domains (Department of the Air Force, forthcoming; U.S. Department of Defense, 2020; Department of the Air Force, 2017).	X	X
	Train against a realistic and modern threat (Wilson and Goldfein, 2019; U.S. Department of Defense, 2020).	X	X
	Train against peer adversary capabilities (training through LVC is the only way to train against certain capabilities) (U.S. Department of Defense, 2020; Department of the Air Force, forthcoming).	X	X
	Test and stress systems in an operationally realistic environment (U.S. Department of Defense, 2020).	X	
	Train in realistic complex environments (including denied or contested EMS environments) (U.S. Department of Defense, 2020; Air Combat Command, 2020b; Department of the Air Force, 2017).	X	X
	Train with a modern mission (Department of the Air Force, 2016).		X

Underlying LVC Technology

We evaluated the state of the art (see Appendix F) and considered the potential for application to meet JADC2 requirements. There are potential and useful applications, including providing training for some of the nontraditional tasks that may be required to implement JADC2, such as building trust in new capabilities, developing faster C2 human-to-human processes, and exploring new tactics for human-machine teaming. However, as with the concept of JADC2, connections with specific tools may be fluid. Given the possibilities and the rapid pace of change as the concept of JADC2 evolves, the USAF should continue to track potentially relevant developments with an eye toward ensuring interoperability. This is particularly true for some of the nontraditional tasks that may otherwise be difficult to train for but are nonetheless necessary for the successful execution of joint all-domain operating concepts.

AOC Operational Systems as Potential for LVC Integration

While the previous section summarizes current and emerging LVC technologies and tools, we now review current and forthcoming capabilities specifically for AOCs. There are multiple AOC systems that could incorporate LVC training tools to enhance JADC2 training and facilitate

JADC2 aspects, such as distributed, resilient C2 and devolution of authorities. A few examples of systems that could integrate with LVC technologies and enhance training at AOCs are listed in Figure 4.1, along with the JADC2 objectives this could address. Note, however, that although these systems may be used in the context of an LVC-supported event or exercise, none of these systems currently has LVC technology incorporated to support training on the system itself. This in turn presents an opportunity for leveraging LVC-related capabilities for improved training. Of the systems noted in Figure 4.1, Block 20 AOC weapon system and ABMS represent opportunities for the DAF to standardize training, as they are meant to be extensively applied across the joint force.

As noted in Figure 4.1, most AOCs employ TBMCS for automated air battle planning and execution management, although the Air Force has started transitioning to the KRADOS. Neither of these systems has LVC capabilities, nor are they planned. However, LVC could and should be considered to enhance training at AOCs.

Command and Control Incident Management Emergency Response Application (C2IMERA), to be employed at AOCs, will enable users to work collaboratively to manage emergency incidents through features like checklists, directives, recalls, customizable dashboards, the conditions board, and the COP and should also be considered to have LVC technologies.[145]

Additionally, the battle management command, control, and communications (C3) is being developed by the Space Development Agency and will provide automated space-based battle management through C2, tasking, mission processing, and dissemination to support time-sensitive kill chain closure at campaign scales.[146]

Currently, the Global Command and Control System—Air Force provides common infrastructure (hardware and software) necessary to pass data among commands, components, and the joint Global Command and Control System.[147] There are opportunities to enhance capabilities of the AOC system, including LVC elements, to positively affect JADC2.

---

[145] Leidos, "Command and Control Incident Management Emergency Response Application (C2IMERA)," fact sheet, undated.

[146] Space Development Agency, "Battle Management Command, Control, and Communication (BMC3)," webpage, undated.

[147] Department of the Air Force, "Presidential Budget," February 2018.

Figure 4.1. Examples of AOC and Enterprise Systems That Could Be Considered to Incorporate LVC

Systems	Description	Does the system currently have LVC?	Training or Operations or Both	Status	Developer	Decentralized C2, dynamic tasking	Potential JADC2 Implications		
							Distributed, resilient C2, devolution of authorities	Faster C2 processes	Inclusion of AI/ML tools for decision support
Kessel Run All Domain Operations Suite (KRADOS)	Future AOC Distributed, Cloud-based C2 System with Open Software (generates ATOs)	No	Operations	Operational at 609 AOC (Al Udeid Air Base, Qatar)	Kessel Run	X	X	X	X
Theater Battle Management Core System (TBMCS)	Current AOC Distributed C2 System (generates ATOs)	No	Both	Operational at AOCs, but being phased out by KRADOS	Lockheed Martin	X	X	X	X
Command and Control Incident Management Emergency Response Application (C2IMERA)	Automated C2 System employing Agile SecDevOps (provides COP, Alerts Personnel, Battle Management)	No	Operations	Disaster Response in US and European Bases, Operational	Leidos, Kessel Run	X	X	X	X
Advanced Battle Management System	Joint C2 System providing sensors, connectivity, effects	No	Operations	In Development, *not operational*	DAF	X	X	X	X
Tranche	Space Battle Management with architecture layers to create a mesh network for information sharing	No	Operations	In Development	Space Development Agency	X	X	X	X
Global Command and Control System – Air Force	a secure, interoperable core command and control constellation	No	Operations	Operational	Air Force Program	X	X	X	X

ABMS

Given the importance of ABMS as a central system for JADC2, in this section, we explore ABMS in more detail. For USAF and U.S. Space Force (USSF), ABMS will help **digitally modernize and connect** the joint and coalition forces and power JADC2 by enabling all echelons to have rapid access to joint capabilities. In addition to enabling the connectedness of the joint force, ABMS will help **enable a data-centric approach to warfare**. As shown in Figure 4.2, ABMS is intended to achieve many of the objectives for executing JADC2.

ABMS has evolved but understanding how the program was originally conceptualized helps break down the multiple different components that could make up the future of ABMS:[148]

1. The ABMS digital infrastructure will move data.
2. This will need to be outed and managed through data tagging, standardization, and merging.
3. The data will be securely processed; this will be particularly challenging, because for JADC2 to achieve success, data security needs to be maintained while allowing all relevant parties to access relevant data.
4. For information to flow in the current information environment, the network will be enabled by a combination of government and commercial connectivity products, which includes software that facilitates connectivity between weapon systems.
5. Software applications are intended to clarify the battlespace with the use of such technologies as AI/ML.
6. Finally, these applications will manage and direct the desired kinetic or nonkinetic effects. These effects can be enabled through machine-to-machine C2, meaning that information could be disseminated across systems without a human in the loop, and systems could be updated or take actions without humans intervening in the process.

Underlying these six elements are digital engineering, open architecture, standards, and concepts.

There are opportunities for the DAF to incorporate training as an element of ABMS, and the DAF should identify opportunities for LVC to enhance ABMS user training.

Developmental Programs That Incorporate LVC Technology for Operational Training

In the preceding material, we discussed AOC systems that lack but might benefit from LVC technology. In this section, we review ongoing DoD-funded R&D training programs that are incorporating LVC technologies, which could respond to the above-referenced deficiencies and could be relevant to training for JADC2. There are ongoing initiatives in DoD to advance LVC technology for operational training, which are shown in Figure 4.2. These LVC technologies do

---

[148] The USAF ABMS Campaign Plan currently guides USAF-concept driven, threat-informed ABMS capability development across the doctrine, organization, training, materiel, leadership, personnel, facilities, and policy (DOTMLPF-P) solutions. HAF A5 ABMS CFT interview with authors.

not include initial skills training (e.g., Pilot Training Next), but they do include current LVC technologies that facilitate force execution. The figure includes LVC technologies, not the infrastructure required to support them (i.e., distributed mission operations or training environments).

Figure 4.2. Ongoing LVC Programs in DoD Used for Operational Training

DoD LVC Program	Brief Description	Warfighting Domain(s) (and Lead)	Training Tier 3/4	Force Generation / Execution	Potential JADC2 Implications			
					Decentralized C2, dynamic tasking	Distributed, resilient C2, devolution of authorities	Faster C2 processes	Inclusion of AI/ML tools for decision support
Airborne Tactical Augmented Reality System (ATARS)	AR in live flight	Air	Tier 4	Force Execution	X		X	
Tactical Combat Training System (TCTS) Increment II (Previously SLATE)	Live flight with constructive elements	Air (Navy Lead, Air Force joined effort and calls it P6CTS)	Tier 4	Force Execution	X		X	X
Hololens	AR HMD	Air, Land, and Sea (Army Lead)	Tier 3,4	Both	X	X	X	

NOTE: This figure shows the use of operational training programs that will incorporate LVC. There are additional systems that use LVC technology for IQT, such as that used by the Undergraduate Pilot Training program. Currently, CCMDs address tiers 1 and 2, and services address tiers 3 and 4. AR = augmented reality; HMD = head-mounted display.

As Figure 4.2 suggests, the current relevant programs focus on force execution and do not tend to the entire C2 chain (tiers 1 through 4). Thus, there is an opportunity for the USAF to ensure future programs capture the full variety of operations from higher headquarters to force execution and force generation. Capturing this spectrum would enable some of the key aspects of JADC2 as discussed, especially decentralized C2 and dynamic tasking. Details of the specific systems follow.

Airborne Tactical Augmented Reality System (ATARS) implements AR in live flight and provides the user with a visual representation of constructive threats. The program is still in development. If ATARS comes to fruition, aircrew will be able to train in an AR environment at high speed and with visually realistic constructive threats. ATARS could be critical to increasing the complexity of training with multiple advanced threats and multidomain warfare. Projecting operational realistic scenarios while in live flight could be instrumental in the success of JADC2, because pilots will be able to practice against threats that they might have not been able to train against—that is, threats they have not encountered in a live environment. In addition, there is potential to simulate a significantly larger number of threats than it would be possible to simulate in live flight.

The **Tactical Combat Training System (TCTS) Increment II** (previously the Secure Live Virtual Constructive Advanced Training [SLATE] program[149]) blends synthetic elements with live participants to simulate high-threat high-density air combat scenarios realistically. Operational complexity is critical to future warfighting, and this system stimulates internal displays that the aviator would view in the cockpit. It is important to note that the pilots will not be able to see the synthetic threats outside the cockpit, but they would be able to see them on the avionic systems in the cockpit.[150] A key attribute of this system is that it is a secure operating framework. Security is a weakness in live training at present because adversaries are able to observe operational training. The combination of open system Multiple Independent Levels of Security (MILS) architecture and government data rights ensures rapid adaptation to emerging threats and missions, while on range or while deployed.[151]

In 2018, Microsoft won a $480 million contract from the Army to develop a mixed-reality headset to help soldiers train, rehearse, and fight.[152] This led to the advancement of the **Hololens**. The technology was developed through a collaborative process that brought Microsoft's user-centric design approach to the military for the first time.[153] The technology will enhance battlespace awareness,[154] which is a key attribute for JADC2.

IT Infrastructure That Supports LVC Technology and Training Systems

Components of the underlying IT infrastructure are fundamental to the LVC-related capabilities we discussed above. Assessing the alignment of LVC capabilities with JADC2 requirements necessitates not just consideration of technical tools and programs but also consideration of fundamental software architectures. Thus, as a central kernel for our review of the state of the art that supports AOC training for JADC2, we present a framework for the major technological components and specify their roles in operational concepts. Although each technological component contributes uniquely to JADC2 activities, each one may also enable

---

[149] SLATE was a program funded in the DAF at the Air Force Research Laboratory but stopped receiving funding in 2019.

[150] The Air Force is also exploring the use of other systems that expand the synthetic capabilities onboard tactical training aircraft, such as the T-7A Red Hawk and Advanced Tactical Trainer.

[151] Formerly diverse requirements for different kinds of systems are now being merged into combined requirements to be met by a single system. To address this trend, a partnership of government, industry, and research institutions are developing the MILS architecture. Although being pursued initially for defense applications, MILS provides a foundation for critical systems of all kinds. Its security, safety, and real-time properties make it suitable for such diverse applications as financial, medical, and critical infrastructures. Rance J. DeLong, "MILS: An Architecture for Security, Safety, and Real Time," Tech Briefs, November 1, 2006; Collins Aerospace, "P6 Combat Training System (CTS)," webpage, undated.

[152] Deborah Bach, "U.S. Army to Use HoloLens Technology in High-Tech Headsets for Soldiers," Microsoft, June 8, 2021.

[153] Bach, 2021.

[154] Bach, 2021.

multiple goals that JADC2 seeks to establish and achieve in practice. Similarly, none of the major technological contributions is specific to JADC2 as a concept. They are independent of JADC2 and are well-established, mature technological state-of-the-art constructs for building large, complex, adaptable computing systems that are designed to scale for such operational challenges as JADC2 and possibly to support LVC capabilities.

To better understand what the goals of JADC2 might imply, Table 4.2 restates the broad goals described in Chapter 2 and provides an IT-oriented perspective on what is to be accomplished and USAF's current plans for implementation.

Table 4.2. An IT Perspective on JADC2 Goals and Its Planned Implementation in USAF

What JADC2 Seeks to Achieve	USAF Planned Implementation
Greater integration of weapon systems for C2 decisions	ABMS
More-fluid flow of data across all operational domains	ABMS
Improved availability of relevant information for C2 decisions	ABMS
Improved C2 decision aids and information workflows	• Data management strategy • Automation incorporating AI/ML
Tactical advantages through expanded edge-C2 capabilities	• Edge computing • Manned-unmanned teaming and UAS • Space systems
Multidomain versatility of jointly deployed or combined forces	• OTTI and LVC • Air, land, and sea interoperability • Space and cyber systems integration
Greater software security of weapon systems	Secure, rapid software development and deployment processes (development, security, and operations [DevSecOps])
Operational advantages through foundational infrastructural changes	• Software factories • Cloud-based computing and infrastructure services • AFWERX

Although broadly stated, each item listed in the left column of Table 4.2 can be associated with an architectural element that fulfills a specific role in the overall system of systems required for JADC2 activities. For example, ABMS is planned to address JADC2 goals for greater weapon systems integration, access to data from all domains, and availability of relevant information for C2 decisionmaking. AI/ML methods will be employed to aid decisionmaking in the context of a data management strategy. Physical systems deployed for edge computing, hybrid human-autonomous systems, and space-related assets are expected to be employed for tactical advantages and C2 capabilities at the tactical edge. OTTI and LVC capabilities, improved multidomain interoperability, and more-direct inclusion of space and cyber systems are expected to improve the effectiveness of activities being executed by jointly deployed and combined forces. Modern software engineering practices, cloud-based infrastructure, and new acquisition processes are being combined with the goal of improving the security and availability of advanced Blue force capabilities.[155]

USAF's efforts related to the ABMS, software factories, Platform One, and Cloud One are expected to contribute as components of USAF's approach for JADC2 implementation. All services are building corresponding capabilities that collectively will enable national security goals for JADC2. However, the ability for independently developed service solutions to merge capabilities is through the use of the JADC2 reference architecture, which sets the driving standard for all future service solutions to be interoperable.[156]

To provide a common picture of critical IT components, we propose the framework shown in Figure 4.3. The diagram provides a structured view, *from an IT perspective*, of the technological capabilities (categories of systems, services, and their roles) being folded into the JADC2 concept. The framework reflects a succinct, structured view of IT components that may further stimulate important coordination across relevant implementation areas and provide support for ongoing discussions across communities (within or external to USAF) that work together to build systems that will ultimately enable JADC2 and related operational concepts.

We focus on the *foundational, large-scale* technological components that are common and necessary for joint all-domain operations to be implemented as envisioned, *independently of specific design decisions*. JADC2 technology infrastructure enables four overarching technical development goals, starting from the bottom layer of Figure 4.3 with the most-foundational elements:

1. operational advantages through foundational infrastructural changes (lowest two layers)
2. expanded software security and application availability (middle three layers)
3. improved C2 decision support with automation (top two layers)
4. expanded C2 capabilities at the edge (multiple layers).

The center of the figure shows five layers (operational users, software applications, etc.); the component technologies listed within them make a distinct operational contribution to JADC2. The shapes next to the layers show the goal(s) supported by that layer—for example, the cloud resources layer is important for three of the four overarching goals. Each layer constitutes a distinct functional aspect of the overarching IT architecture that enables the implementation of JADC2 capabilities.

The high-level foundational presentation in Figure 4.3 provides a succinct, contextual view of IT components, while more-detailed architectural views and specific capabilities are being articulated by USAF and JADC2 cross-functional teams (CFTs).[157] Given the USAF's strategic

---

[155] *Blue force* denotes friendly forces, as opposed to *Red force*, which denotes opposing or adversary forces.

[156] Comment provided by HAF A5 ABMS CFT interview with authors.

[157] For example, the USAF Rapid Capabilities Office outlines six categories of technological capability centered on secure processing, connectivity, data management, applications, sensor integration, and effects integration, each

objectives and an overall view of what may be required, the major groupings of IT components needed to support JADC2 and how they are captured in the proposed framework are summarized below.

Operational advantages through foundational infrastructural changes. High-availability physical infrastructure and facilities and an advanced foundation for communications and computing are emphasized in the foundational infrastructure layers. Technological changes to infrastructure in the cloud resources and data center layers directly affect the variety of capabilities provided to the USAF enterprise for JADC2 concepts.[158]

Expanded software security and application availability. A flexible, common foundation for secure software development and application availability is enabled by three layers: software applications, platform, and cloud resources. They provide advanced integrated data architectures, analytics, and software services. The platform layer focuses on normalized, secure software development environments and tools. The software applications layer emphasizes the integration of information, and it includes corresponding capability advances on the edge systems themselves.[159]

Improved C2 decision support with automation. The entire IT enterprise and the systems comprising it support JADC2 operators and edge systems as its "users." These include tactical C2 and operational C2 operators who are expected to use new operational capabilities for data services, planning, and decisions with input from all domains. JADC2 systems, such as ABMS, will provide C2 decision aids (e.g., automatic generation of courses of action) and an ability to rapidly process large volumes of data from multidomain assets to inform decisions.

Expanded C2 capabilities at the edge. Edge systems are represented twice in Figure 4.3 for simplicity, but JADC2 edge systems will rely on new networking and computing infrastructure as well as software services positioned higher in the stack. Edge systems for JADC2 will require new physical links over tactical networks, newer protocols for communication, and tactical capabilities for computational tasks capable of supporting operational activities in contested, degraded, and denied operating environments. Such systems are expected to enable tactical C2, including human-machine teaming, to create a warfighting advantage.

The bottom bar shows that the joint staff and each service are actively making contributions to JADC2 as a concept and in their respective domains. The Army is conducting experiments that are increasingly joint in character and complex in implementation through Project

---

encompassing multiple related enabling capabilities that leverage various aspects of the envisioned USAF technology infrastructure. See Theresa Hitchens, "ABMS Grows Up: Air Force Shifts Focus to Delivering Kit," *Breaking Defense*, May 24, 2021d.

[158] *Cloud computing* is a computational strategy to leverage distributed computational resources. It uses a potentially dynamic and highly heterogenous mixture of computing resources under variable operational conditions for computing and information processing. Therefore, it offers an advantage for USAF and JADC2 in general. Cloud One helps to achieve that advantage by providing the technical capabilities to leverage computing resources.

[159] USAF's Platform One is designed to use Cloud One capabilities. Block 20 solutions and ABMS-enabling software components manifest in the middle layer, alongside cross-service and joint software systems.

Convergence. Similarly, the Navy and Marine Corps are establishing equivalent maritime capabilities through Project Overmatch. The main body of Figure 4.3 (above the bar) is applicable in all these efforts: The primary IT components contributing to joint all-domain operations are shared across them.

Figure 4.3. An IT Perspective on the Technological Components Enabling JADC2 Capabilities

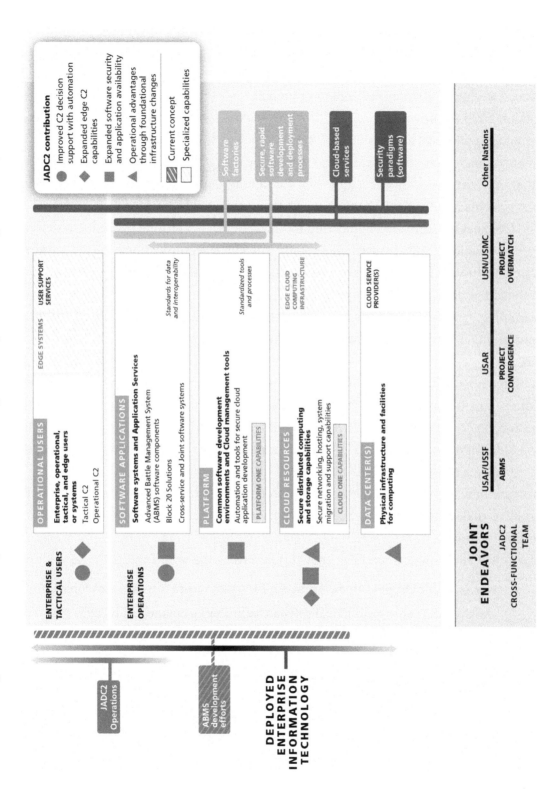

NOTE: USAR = U.S. Army Reserve; USMC = U.S. Marine Corps; USN = U.S. Navy.

67

DevSecOps—Implications for Training

DevSecOps is a critical underlying aspect of IT and software development. In this section, we review this method for secure, rapid software development and deployment. This method has significant implications for the large-scale capabilities development that is necessary for achieving the overarching JADC2 goals.

Since October 2020, the DevSecOps approach has been promoted by DoD policy with DoD Instruction 5000.87, *Operation of the Software Acquisition Pathway*, and is viewed as an important technological aspect of JADC2 infrastructure to facilitate secure, rapid software development and deployment processes (see Figure 4.4).[160] In this section, we look briefly at the potential implications of this new approach for rapidly developing secure software in AOC weapon systems and for the LVC training systems expected to train AOC operators.

The DevSecOps software engineering method was chosen for its potential to deliver software securely and rapidly. DoD Instruction 5000.87 introduces approved options for acquiring software capabilities for weapon systems across the department. Presently, DevSecOps is being implemented to develop and deploy new AOC weapon systems at selected AOCs. However, many training systems relevant to AOC operations also rely on software-based capabilities to deliver training and are not included in the software development process for the new weapon systems.

With the new policy, DoD's intent is to prescribe "procedures for the establishment of software acquisition pathways to provide for the efficient and effective acquisition, development, integration, and timely delivery of secure software in accordance with the requirements of Section 800 of Public Law 116-92"[161] and "to modernize its software practices to provide the agility to deliver resilient software at the speed of relevance."[162]

Because new software capabilities are a core aspect of JADC2 development activities, it is important to understand what DevSecOps means in practice and its potential implications for future LVC training systems.

The DoD Chief Information Officer (CIO) describes the term *DevSecOps* as follows:[163]

> DevSecOps is the industry best practice for rapid, secure software development.
>
> DevSecOps is an organizational software engineering culture and practice that aims at unifying software development (Dev), security (Sec) and operations

---

[160] The DevSecOps method is actively being pursued by the Air Force, Navy, and Army for software implementations.

[161] DoD Instruction 5000.87, 2020, p. 1.

[162] U.S. Department of Defense, *DoD Enterprise DevSecOps Reference Design: CNCF Kubernetes*, Version 2.0, March 2021, p. 7.

[163] DoD CIO, "DoD Enterprise DevSecOps Reference Design 1.0 Public Release," September 12, 2019. The methodologies for agile software development and DevSecOps are closely linked. DevSecOps incorporates security directly into software development and deployment, whereas software security may be addressed subsequently to an agile process.

(Ops). The main characteristic of DevSecOps is to automate, monitor, and apply security at all phases of the software lifecycle: plan, develop, build, test, release, deliver, deploy, operate, and monitor. In DevSecOps, testing and security are shifted to the left through automated unit, functional, integration, and security testing—this is a key DevSecOps differentiator since security and functional capabilities are tested and built simultaneously.

Fundamentally, DevSecOps is an engineering method emphasizing the secure and rapid development and deployment of software throughout the software life cycle.[164] DevSecOps ensures a close partnership between software developer teams and AOC operators. The software development teams implement secure, streamlined software practices while delivering new capabilities, and AOC operators receive incremental, operationally relevant advances to operational systems. When combined, the approach can support an advantageous execution of AOC missions.

For the purposes of the training-focused discussion here, these benefits are not sufficient, and additional considerations warrant attention. This is because DevSecOps also affects the concurrency of training systems with operational systems in two ways.[165] First, when new functionality is deployed into an AOC's production environment for operational use, existing training systems cannot immediately replicate the AOC capability in the training environment. Second, trainers are not able to update the training process to incorporate operational changes arising from introduced functionality until they become aware of it. A corresponding challenge arises from the different acquisition methods applied for training systems and software introduced via DevSecOps for new AOC weapon systems. Software changes to existing training systems will be difficult to synchronize with new operational capabilities because the training software updates are developed on a separate timeline and the DevSecOps method delivers system changes at a quicker pace. This raises the specter of training capabilities falling even more dramatically behind the current operational environment than is presently the case. Moreover, some of the capabilities under discussion for inclusion, such as AI/ML tools for decisionmaking, require end-user comfort to employ—that is, their implementation requires training. Consideration of these issues is key to ensuring that training is able to facilitate the fast implementation of various improvements rather than posing an unexpected barrier.

---

[164] For example, the Carnegie Mellon University Software Engineering Institute defines *DevSecOps* as: "a set of principles and practices that provide faster delivery of secure software capabilities by improving the collaboration and communication between software development teams, IT operations, and security staff within an organization, as well as with acquirers, suppliers, and other stakeholders in the life of a software system." Carnegie Mellon University Software Engineering Institute, "DevSecOps," webpage, undated.

[165] AOC personnel, multiple discussions about DevSecOps with the authors, December 2020 and February–August 2021.

Distributed Training Systems

Numerous distributed systems relevant to all-domain training either exist today or are in development, and these systems can help support training for JADC2. There is an opportunity to leverage existing or forthcoming systems without having to reinvent them. Thus, whereas in previous sections, we assessed more-fundamental LVC-related technologies, AOC software systems, and DoD R&D programs, in this section, we evaluate distributed training systems with respect to applicability to LVC training for JADC2. Table 4.3 compares their contribution to C2 training for joint, all-domain operations.[166] In the discussion that follows, relationships between existing and emerging systems are reviewed.

Table 4.3. Comparison of the C2 Training Contribution of Existing and Emerging Distributed Systems Relevant to JADC2 Training

System or Environment	Status	JADC2 Focused	C2 Training	Joint or Cross-Service Capabilities	Joint Training Capabilities	Joint Training Tier	Organization
ABMS	In development	Yes	No	Yes	No	N/A	Air Force
AOC Block 20	In development	Yes	No	Yes	No	N/A	Air Force
ACE-IOS	Deployed	Yes	Yes	Yes	Yes	2–3	Air Force
AFMSTT	Deployed	Yes	Yes	Yes	Yes	2–3	Air Force
BLCSE	Deployed	Yes	Yes	Yes	No	N/A	Army
C2SET	In development	Yes	Yes	Yes	Yes	1–4	Air Force
CSTE	Concept	No	No	Yes	Yes	4	Air Force
JLCCTC	Deployed	No	Yes	Yes	Yes	2–4	Army
JLVC	Deployed	No	Yes	Yes	Yes	1–3	Joint Staff J7
JSE	Initial deployment	No	No	Yes	Yes	4	Navy/Air Force
JTSE	In development	Yes	Yes	Yes	Yes	1–4	Joint Staff J7
PMTEC	Concept	Yes	Yes	Yes	Yes	1–4	INDOPACOM

NOTE: Currently, CCMDs address tiers 1 and 2, and services address tiers 3 and 4. ACE-IOS = Air and Space Cyber Constructive Environment—Information Operations Simulator; AFMSTT = Air Force Modeling and Simulation Training Toolkit; BLCSE = Battle Lab Collaborative Simulation Environment; C2SET = Command and Control Synthetic Environment for Training; CSTE = Common Synthetic Training Environment; JSE = Joint Simulation Environment; JTSE = Joint Training Synthetic Environment; JLVC = Joint Live Virtual Constructive; JLCCTC = Joint Land Component Constructive Training Capability; N/A = not applicable; PMTEC = Pacific Multi-Domain Test and Experimentation Capability.

All the systems listed in Table 4.3 contribute to joint capabilities for joint readiness. AOC Block 20 systems primarily focus on new operational systems for AOC activities. Although central to the Air Force's contribution to JADC2, ABMS is not a training system and does not

---

[166] Table 4.3 focuses on distributed systems used by the Air Force and corresponding joint training systems for comparison.

intrinsically support JADC2 training.[167] Several systems offer potential for JADC2 training, but they are just preliminary concepts or in development and may not presently focus on JADC2 strategy. These include the Air Force's Common Synthetic Training Environment (CSTE),[168] the Navy-led Joint Simulation Environment (JSE),[169] JS J7's Joint Training Synthetic Environment (JTSE),[170] and INDOPACOM's Pacific Multi-Domain Test and Experimentation Capability (PMTEC).[171]

Existing distributed training systems include the family of systems in the Air, Space, and Cyber Constructive Environment (ASCCE)—Information Operations Simulator (ACE-IOS), JS J7's Joint Live Virtual Constructive (JLVC) federation, and the Army's Joint Land Component Constructive Training Capability (JLCCTC) and its Battle Lab Collaborative Simulation Environment (BLCSE). These systems are deployed and are actively used for distributed, joint training exercises across training tiers applicable to JADC2 or for experimentation, test, and evaluation in the case of BLCSE.

ACE-IOS is a suite of federation-based training capabilities and is the Air Force's primary system for joint training exercises.[172] The Air Force is evolving and redeveloping ACE-IOS as the Command and Control Synthetic Environment for Training (C2SET).[173] In parallel, the Air Force and Navy are pursuing advanced, synthetic tactical training environments targeting fifth generation (and beyond) platforms. These are the CSTE and the JSE, respectively.

C2SET seeks to align new AOC weapon systems (e.g., those developed by Kessel Run teams) with modeling and simulation training systems and will be based on the Advanced Framework for Simulation, Integration and Modeling (AFSIM).[174] The system was necessitated

---

[167] Although ABMS is not a training system, a warfighter requirement capability for human capital development is specified in the ABMS campaign plan to analyze and address training needs for ABMS. HAF A5 ABMS CFT interview with authors.

[168] Meredith Roaten, Air Force Looking to Boost Connectivity for Simulators," *National Defense Magazine*, July 22, 2021.

[169] Jeremy S. Smith, "Joint Simulation Environment," Naval Air Systems Command, NAVAIR public release 2018-356, 2018; Timothy Menke, "Joint Simulation Environment for United States Air Force Test Support," *NATO Science and Technology Organization Meeting Proceedings*, STO-MP-MSG-171-17, October 18, 2019.

[170] "Alion Awarded $73 Million Task Order to Provide Joint Training Synthetic Environment Research and Development," PR Newswire, October 13, 2020.

[171] Jason Sherman, "DOD Eyes $2.7 Billion Proposal to Wrap Half the Planet in Multidomain Test Range," *Inside Defense*, April 8, 2020.

[172] Software federations comprise heterogenous, distributed simulation systems relying on a single communications framework for the exchange of relevant information during training exercises.

[173] Air Force Agency for Modeling and Simulation (AFAMS), discussion with the authors, and review of related source material, July 20, 2021.

[174] Kessel Run team, discussion with the authors, August 25, 2021.

by the introduction of KRADOS[175] as a replacement for the TBMCS, which created a concurrency gap between training capability built on TBMCS and the new weapon system.[176] Concurrently with closing this gap, C2SET will incorporate training capabilities presently delivered by ACE-IOS systems, will improve on them by expanding their technological foundation to address limitations in the existing training tools, and will modernize the development and delivery of training capabilities. C2SET includes modeling components, such as the Air Force Modeling and Simulation Training Toolkit (AFMSTT) and the Air Warfare Simulation. Critically, C2SET integrates *training* needs into the scope of the DevSecOps implementations for AOC weapon systems, and it bridges an emerging gap between Kessel Run–developed and –deployed applications and existing training capabilities. However, potential interoperability gaps exist between C2SET and environments, such as CSTE and JS J7's JTSE, as depicted in Figure 4.4. C2SET, CSTE, and JTSE are being developed independently of each other and address different aspects of training. CSTE is centrally focused on advanced, tactical air training in a synthetic environment that is centrally managed.

JTSE is currently premised on JLVC (a decentralized federation environment), the architecture of which is expected to evolve to provide centrally managed common data services for all DoD services.[177] The joint training environment will support various training tiers across multiple domains, like JLVC does, but how C2SET will integrate into the environment and interoperate with other simulations is yet unclear. Similarly, there are other joint explorations of Air Force and Army air space deconfliction systems that seek to use *existing* training capabilities for better integration with Army capabilities with such initiatives as the Defense Advanced Research Projects Agency's Air Space Total Awareness for Rapid Tactical Execution (ASTARTE) program.[178] However, no link between ASTARTE and C2SET is presently specified.

---

[175] Carrie Volpe, "609th AOC Optimizes ATO Production, First to Use KRADOS Operationally," U.S. Air Force, May 7, 2021; Bruce Katz and Peter Ising, "Kessel Run Deploys KRADOS to Air Operations Center," Kessel Run, January 12, 2021.

Other Kessel Run–deployed applications include a tanker planning system, called Jigsaw, and Slapshot, the new MAAP builder.

[176] "Lockheed Martin Tasked to Integrate Battle Management Capabilities for USAF's KRADOS," *Military & Aerospace Electronics*, June 3, 2021.

[177] John Dvorak, Roy Scrudder, Kevin Gupton, and Kevin Hellman, "Enabling Joint Synthetic Training Interoperability Through Joint Federated Common Data Services," *Cybersecurity & Information Systems Information Analysis Center Journal*, Vol. 7, No. 3, 2020.

[178] Theresa Hitchens, "DARPA Builds AI to Avoid Army, AF Fratricide," *Breaking Defense*, February 17, 2021c.

Figure 4.4. Emerging and Existing Training Systems

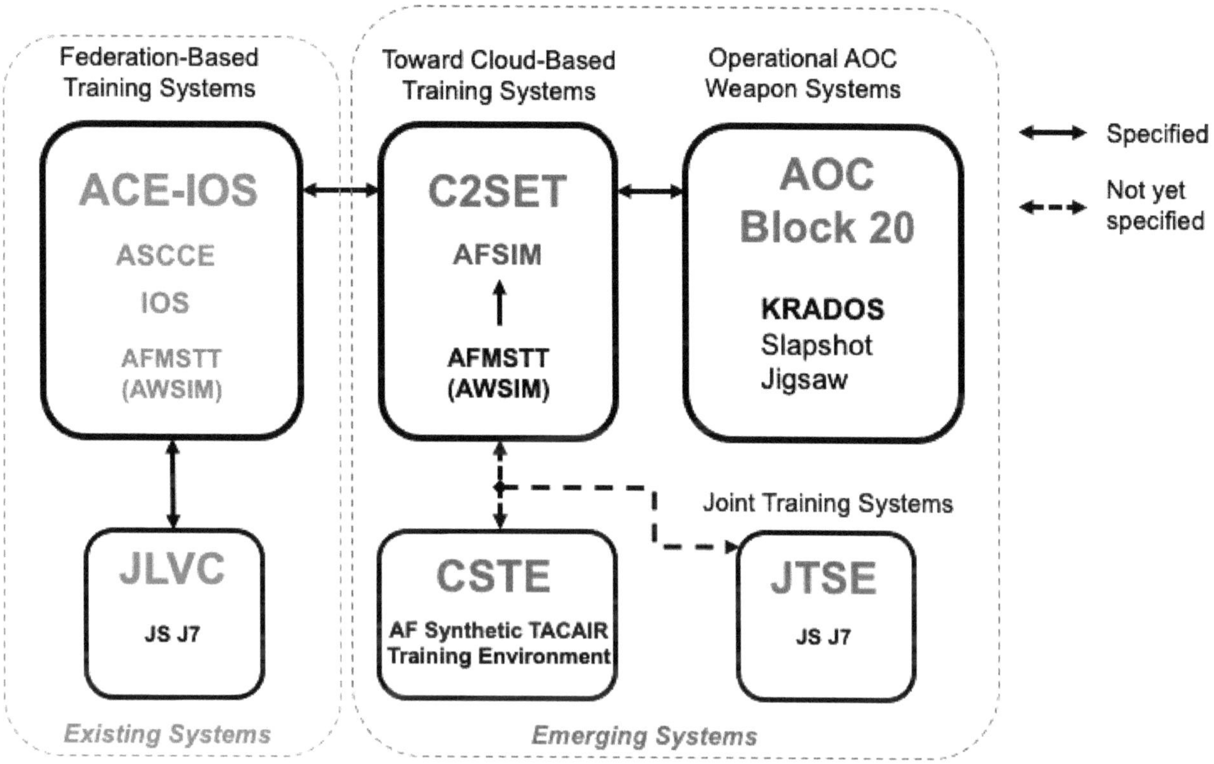

NOTE: TACAIR = tactical air.

CSTE is a line of effort in the Air Force's emerging Synthetic Test and Training Capability plan.[179] It seeks to develop an advanced, synthetic tactical training infrastructure focused on fifth-generation systems (and beyond) with support for multiplatform training that intends to provide or enable the following:

- a platform-agnostic, scalable, and centralized training infrastructure
- greater distributed-mission training across multiple, next-generation platforms simultaneously
- expanded representation of operationally relevant electromagnetic operating environments)
- representation for a greater variety of potential threats not possible to train on existing infrastructure and environments.

---

[179] Project materials provided by AFAMS. Also see the following National Training and Simulation Association (NTSA) Simulation Training and Community Forum presentations: Nick Yates, "OTTI Update: Synthetic Test and Training Capability," presentation, NTSA Simulation Training and Community Forum, August 11, 2021; Kevin McFarland, "Digital Engineering Shift and Simulation Vision: Common Synthetic Environment," NTSA Simulation Training and Community Forum, August 11, 2021.

CSTE will also leverage digital engineering and model-based simulation engineering for realistic synthetic presentations of warfighting capabilities.[180] As part of the design, cloud computing services will deliver effects to distributed training participants in real time, improving the Air Force's current training capabilities to systematically inject more realism into tactical training.

However, the designs for both C2SET and CSTE leave open the mechanisms by which they will integrate to the larger-force training exercises necessary for JADC2 training. This exposes a potential gap between these emerging LVC training capabilities and an interoperability challenge. Both C2SET and CSTE prioritize enhancements to air domain training more than space and cyber with the risk of providing partial or inadequate training in these domains.

In summary, existing LVC training systems are being employed for JADC2 demonstrations. They can provide a preexisting basis for models that must also be present in training capabilities for new, JADC2-oriented operational systems. However, integrating these models into training capabilities based on new operational systems will require a systematic approach to avoid incipient interoperability issues.

Space and Cyber Synthetic Environments

Much of the discussion thus far has centered on the air domain. However, given the all-domain aspect of JADC2 and the relatively new demands on space and cyber from organizational and training perspectives, we provide a close look at training issues and risks with these domains from a technical perspective while considering LVC training environments. Presently, both space and cyber effects are viewed as supporting training exercises rather than being an integral part of training exercises.[181] Both domains require specialized expertise and have faced resource challenges in the past, limiting the effectiveness of capabilities for training and readiness.[182]

Space capabilities are viewed as critical to JADC2 execution.[183] The recent series of Global Information Dominance Experiments (GIDE) rely on space-based assets for situational awareness to demonstrate JADC2 capabilities.[184] The GIDE iterations are spin-offs from ABMS

---

[180] Roaten, 2021.

[181] USSF representatives, discussion with the authors, September 20, 2021; U.S. Space Command (SPACECOM), July 12, 2021.

[182] Air Force Space Command, *Air Force Space Command Live Virtual Constructive—Operations Training Review Report*, October 7, 2016.

[183] Theresa Hitchens, "Esper Orders SDA to Link C2 Networks for All-Domain Ops," Defense News, May 6, 2020a; U.S. Department of Defense, *Command, Control, and Communications (C3) Modernization Strategy*, September 2020a.

[184] Abraham Mahshie, "VanHerck: SPACECOM 'Critical' to Latest High-Tech Exercise, but Hurdles Remain, *Air & Space Forces Magazine*, July 28, 2021.

on-ramps, which enable strategic-level analysis of JADC2 execution, involving all the CCMDs and including initial assessments of space capabilities.[185] GIDE demonstrated automated course-of-action selection and sensor-to-shooter execution. The automated C2 processes were broadly informed by large volumes of globally collected data from heterogenous sources that identified emerging situations rapidly and recommended strategies for commanders to deter escalation or prepare forces for additional actions should escalation occur.[186]

However, to provide sustained training and experimentation in a synthetic space training environment, foundational data will be needed through direct use of operational data or operationally validated synthetic data. Because space domain training frequently relies on the use of live assets, synthetic training environments, such as the Space Test and Training Range, will enable testing and training with on-orbit assets in a secure setting for a variety of emerging threats to space-based assets.[187]

All-domain cyber training environments are in initial stages of implementation and deployment. The 16th AF is responsible for both cyberspace operations and intel operations. Air Force Cyber reports to U.S. Cyber Command (CYBERCOM), and the Cyber Command and Control Mission System is the primary Air Force cyber weapon system.[188] Cyber training systems are being developed for collective use by services as part of the Joint Cyber Warfighting Architecture (JCWA), led by CYBERCOM. The JCWA comprises five main components, of which one is the Persistent Cyber Training Environment (PCTE).[189] The Army is the lead developer for PCTE, and its primary users are CYBERCOM and other services. For cyber domain activities, partnerships are seen as key, and recently, CYBERCOM has entered an agreement with the Australian Defence Force to develop a cyber training range.[190]

The cyber domain has offensive and defensive components. Defensive components focus on mitigations for adversarial activities against Air Force operational capabilities, especially infrastructure and systems. In contrast, offensive operations generate and apply cyber effects to project force in the cyber and other domains, in direct opposition to adversarial actions, for the explicit purpose of establishing a warfighting advantage. Cyber operations themselves (defensive and offensive) are premised on the potential exploitation of technological vulnerabilities present in a system (or collection of systems) for adversarial gain.

---

[185] SPACECOM representative, discussion with the authors, July 12, 2021.

[186] USSF representative, discussion with the authors, September 20, 2021.

[187] Courtney Albon, "Space Force Crafting Requirements for National Space and Test Training Range," *Inside Defense*, January 21, 2021a; Courtney Albon, "AFRL, Space Force Set Priorities for New Testing Enterprise," *Inside Defense*, February 3, 2021b.

[188] Air Combat Command, "Cyber Command and Control Mission System (C3MS)," webpage, January 24, 2020a.

[189] Mark Pomerleau, "US Cyber Command Advances on Platform to Consolidate Its Myriad Tools and Data," C4ISRNET, November 2, 2020.

[190] U.S. Cyber Command, "US and Australia Sign First-Ever Cyber Agreement to Develop Virtual Training Range," December 4, 2020.

Cyber domain training also requires an extensive understanding of the technical implementation of an operational system, how to select effective tools and implement exploits or countermeasures, and how exploits affect activities in an operational environment. Therefore, test environments to assess cyber vulnerabilities of a system (or systems) also provide a unique baseline for training capabilities (defensive or offensive).[191] That is, there is a unique opportunity to develop OTTI for cyber training in close conjunction with cyberspace testing infrastructure.

Several issues affecting how space and cyber training environments are implemented arose during discussions with AOC, DAF, USSF, and SPACECOM officials. Table 4.4 summarizes the issues and potential risks stemming from them, should they go unaddressed. Without a dedicated synthetic training environment for the space domain, training risks remaining at the status quo and providing inadequate training for expected future threats and tactics. A space training environment will require funding to support the development of operationally valid and foundational data along with the ability to model space capabilities in large-scale force training exercises. Similarly, cyber domain training will require models capable of training on advanced cyber tactics to be integrated with larger-force training exercises. Providing partial or insufficient cyber training capabilities may yield a false picture of force readiness and limited understanding of the impact of Red and Blue tactics.

---

[191] Vincent E. Urias, Brian V. Leeuwen, William M. S. Stout, and Han W. Lin, "Dynamic Cybersecurity Training Environments for an Evolving Cyber Workforce," *2017 IEEE International Symposium on Technology for Homeland Security Proceedings*, 2017; William M. S. Stout, Vincent Urias, Brian P. Van Leeuwen, and Han Wei Lin, "Dynamic Cybersecurity Training Environments for an Evolving Cyber Workforce," Sandia National Laboratories, SAND2017-2452C, March 1, 2017.

Table 4.4. Space and Cyber Domain Synthetic Training Environments—Training Issues and Risks

Training Domain	Training Issues	Risks
Space	• Large quantities of structured, operationally relevant space data are inaccessible for training. • Allocation of space-based assets for input to training exercises relies on allocation of live systems. • The role and character of space domain assets are not well understood by AOC operators. • Synthetic datasets require operationally valid data and the translation of unstructured data to be approved for use in training. • Space effects are incorporated in larger-force training exercises but are not a core part of training environments. • Space models are well understood but are not implemented for use in training to the extent that is necessary. • A synthetic environment with sufficient funding is not available for use in training and testing on-orbit systems in secure, dedicated, space-specific infrastructure that includes distributed computing capabilities.	• Accessibility to structured, operationally relevant data limits modeling and simulation capabilities for space domain training. • White-carding of space effects is preferred during AOC training. • C2 training involving space-based assets is limited by the rudimentary knowledge AOC operators have of space systems. • Space-based assets and functions are not represented or articulated sufficiently enough to demonstrate existing or future tactics, reducing training capabilities to develop and assess space-based TTP for JADC2. • Space-based events, for instance, on-orbit interactions with other space-based assets (friendly or otherwise), are not simulated well enough to explore the impact of resulting effects for JADC2 missions.
Cyber	• Models for advanced cyber tactics and behaviors require more than system-specific, technical knowledge about how a system operates in performing its intended functions. • Cyber effects are disruptive to goals of larger-force training exercises. • Cyber effects are incorporated in larger-force training exercises but are not yet a core part of training environments. • Cyber test and training systems share very similar technical needs, but cyber training and test environments are not necessarily designed with a shared baseline.	• Not including cyber effects will limit JADC2 training for command-level decisionmaking in disrupted, degraded, and denied environments. • Partial but insufficient representation of cyber tactics prohibits realistic assessments of their impact on execution of tasks resulting from tactical C2 decisions. • Inadequate modeling of cyber tactics (including timing-based attacks) and resulting effects creates a false picture of force readiness and the effectiveness of Blue and Red capabilities. • OTTI for synthetic test and training systems might diverge in the capabilities provided, yielding conflicting assessments of readiness.

Conclusion

This chapter provided an assessment of LVC capabilities, software, and programs with respect to their relevance to JADC2, while leveraging the requirements outlined in Chapter 2 as a basis for evaluation. This work rounds out the analysis of training needs and how processes and capabilities align with those needs. In this chapter, we began by reviewing the perceived value of LVC in DoD and the DAF. We then reviewed available LVC technologies for their potential contributions to JADC2 training environments. Next, a structured perspective on the IT components planned for use with JADC2 was introduced. The resulting framework exposes the important aspects of IT that will be required to implement JADC2 and how those technologies contribute to JADC2 goals. The framework also provides a mechanism for facilitating a common understanding of JADC2 aspects and capabilities. We provided a brief discussion on DoD's and the DAF's recent adoption of DevSccOps as an engineering method for software acquisition, highlighting both operational benefits and potential training concerns. Next, we evaluated existing and emerging distributed training systems with respect to their ability to support training for JADC2. The chapter concluded with a summarization of LVC training issues and potential risks for training space and cyber domain operators.

A key theme throughout this chapter was the necessity to align acquisition with underlying needs. Especially as more R&D is funded by industry rather than government, despite the best intentions laid out in DoD technology and training road maps, there is a risk of capabilities advancing independently from specific training needs, such as those related to JADC2. Thus, emerging capabilities must be assessed relative to training needs that then align with operational needs. This process should continue and repeat over time as technology and military operations change. With respect to technology, JADC2 will drive more-complex and more-networked training, and there is a risk of the siloed development of supporting distributed training systems. Yet, there are many existing or developing capabilities from which to draw and avoid such siloes. With respect to operations, space and cyber represent the latest frontier, and there is an opportunity to be proactive about using LVC to help support training in these domains as related operational concepts mature.

Key findings for this chapter are as follows:

- **Interoperability across the air, space, and cyber domains is a substantial challenge** for emerging JADC2 systems and LVC training environments. Multidomain operations introduce a high degree of complexity beyond the capabilities of existing training systems. Thus, new LVC training capabilities must be considered directly alongside the development of JADC2 operational systems.
- **LVC technologies are advancing rapidly in the commercial sector** with respect to their ability to support distributed, real-time, collaborative interactions, so the USAF should keep a pulse on the LVC commercial market for emerging cost-effective training solutions. In addition, the USAF should leverage commercial LVC technologies to incorporate distributed training in support of distributed C2 execution.
- **LVC training tools can be used for training on nontraditional tasks**, such as building trust in new capabilities, developing faster C2 human-to-human processes, and exploring new tactics for human-machine teaming.
- **Synthetic training environments can support training on decentralized execution** and the greater need for battlespace awareness arising from multidomain operations.
- **Unless LVC training systems are directly incorporated** in the scope of software development for weapon systems, the new DevSecOps acquisition approach will complicate the concurrency gap between training capabilities and operational systems.
- **Expand joint partnerships** to develop JADC2 systems that are designed for interoperability from their inception. Numerous JADC2 efforts are taking place in parallel across DoD, and joint demonstrations of emerging JADC2 capabilities are being executed. However, none of the efforts share a sufficiently common, well-defined

architecture to support mutual development of JADC2 systems that are complementary in function and composable depending on the type of potential conflict.

- **Space and cyber domains are viewed as critical for JADC2**, but neither is adequately represented in AOC training exercises nor in emerging USAF LVC training environments.

- **Space and cyber operations require specialized resources** that are supported by dedicated synthetic training environments and prioritize all-domain operations. Space training relies substantially on live assets without an ability to train adequately for potential threats. Cyber operations require a detailed ability to study the operational impacts of both offensive and defensive tactics.

- **Cyber domain test and training environments share a common baseline**, presenting a unique opportunity to develop training infrastructure for cyber operations in close conjunction with test infrastructure cyber operations. Because both cyber training and testing require a detailed technical understanding of the operational design of a system and its potential vulnerabilities, this overlap can be leveraged to develop training environments based on existing test environments.

Chapter 5. AOC-Specific Analysis and Assessment of LVC for Supporting JADC2 Training

Given the assessment of training needs, processes, and capabilities in Chapters 2 through 4, this chapter provides an analysis to highlight any opportunities for improvement across the AOCs and a summary of how LVC can support training for JADC2. A key aspect of our approach is the mapping of training needs to training capabilities and then to training processes. In this chapter, we aggregate the more detailed analyses from previous chapters to summarize the results of this process and illustrate how LVC may support JADC2 training across the AOCs.

First, using documentation and extensive discussions with personnel from each AOC regarding the emerging JADC2 concept, we describe the more detailed comparison process for cross-AOC consideration of (1) training needs at each AOC, (2) the available training pipelines and CT opportunities, and (3) information about the current and planned technological capabilities. We describe the coding and compilation of a comparison matrix, revealing any gaps or potential duplication. Although the intent of the preceding chapters has been to identify contextual and overarching issues, in this chapter, we focus on aggregating and analyzing AOC-specific data. We then summarize previously discussed analysis to outline a road map of how LVC can help support AOC training for JADC2.

Although we find that LVC can help support the complex training JADC2 will require, LVC resources can take time to develop and mature, and they require a strategic outlook. Thus, we compare the status quo with the envisioned JADC2 future to consider where LVC may best contribute. This picture represents a snapshot in time, as JADC2 and its implementation are still in development. Nonetheless, we seek to answer the question, given what we know now, of how can LVC best help support the USAF as it implements JADC2. And, more specifically, what might be needed with respect to LVC capabilities to enable the USAF to support JADC2's current and envisioned capabilities?

AOC Comparison Matrix

Our study focused on the heart of C2 in the USAF—the AOC. As noted in Chapter 3, AOCs vary with respect to how JADC2 is implemented and how training is conducted, and thus vary with respect to the most effective use of LVC. A key element of understanding this issue is a consideration of the similarities among and variation across AOCs. Thus, we created a matrix with which to compare AOCs (regarding needs, processes, and capabilities) and identify pervasive themes.

Method

Our study ideal was to consider USAF C2 training as it will be several years after JADC2 is implemented. Ideally, a consideration of requisite training requires a conceptualization and understanding of the job to be trained, provided by job analysis. In this case, the actual jobs could require drastic changes to the status quo, and the relevant concepts are still under development. Thus, even a future-oriented job analysis procedure, such as that described by Landis, Fogli, and Goldberg (1998), would be difficult to undertake.[192] Nonetheless, our approach incorporates elements of job analysis, such as a consideration of relevant tasks undertaken at the operational level for JADC2, supplementing the examination of existing task lists noted in Chapter 2, as well as some consideration of the current job of C2 operators at the AOC. Ultimately, to fully implement JADC2 at the AOC and facilitate training, the Air Force may need to consider the quantitative assessment of human behavior, such as measures of cognitive workload while performing assigned tasks. Simultaneously, quantitative assessment of mission-technical measures and outcomes must be conducted, which will enable a determination of the effectiveness of training undertaken. The effectiveness of training systems can be determined by comparing cognitive workload and mission performance. Trainee learning curves can be characterized with regard to readiness when mission tasks can be executed without errors, at high levels of proficiency, and at low levels of cognitive workload.[193]

As noted, our approach to this analysis involved extensive interviews across the AOCs. During our study, the Air Force was implementing the new career field of 13O, or Multi-Domain Warfare Officers who are intended to be operational-level experts who can incorporate multiple warfighting domains and fill some of the perceived gap in this capability.[194] They are in a sense key SMEs as their training is designed to facilitate JADC2. In our interviews, we spoke to some of these officers, many of whom are billeted at AOCs. However, they were not our sole focus: We also spoke to many other SMEs in current C2 and training at the various geographic and global AOCs to get a sense of the status quo and how the SMEs anticipated it might change to accommodate JADC2.

During the analysis of AOC training and in our discussions with these personnel, we were seeking information regarding three primary areas: what types of training would be required under JADC2, what the current training processes are, and what technological capabilities are currently available or under development. We took extensive notes during these discussions,

---

[192] Ronald S. Landis, Lawrence Fogli, and Edie Goldberg, "Future-Oriented Job Analysis: A Description of the Process and Its Organizational Implications," *International Journal of Selection and Assessment*, Vol. 6, No. 3, 1998.

[193] Amy Dideriksen, Christopher Reuter, Thomas Patry, Thomas Schnell, Jaclyn Hoke, and Jocelyn Faubert, "Define Expert: Characterizing Proficiency for Physiological Measures of Cognitive Workload," *Proceedings of the Interservice/Industry Training, Simulation, and Education Conference*, December 2018.

[194] U.S. Air Force Personnel Center, *Air Force Officer Classification Directory (AFOCD): The Official Guide to the Air Force Officer Classification Codes*, October 31, 2021.

which were organized by AOC. After organizing and cleaning the notes, they were reviewed for general themes relevant to the topics under investigation and coded. The nine codes defined in Table 5.1 were applied to key portions of the notes. Given the ambiguity regarding the implementation of JADC2 at present, our approach should be considered exploratory.

Table 5.1. Coding Scheme for AOC Notes

Code	Definition
Mission	Current missions and day-to-day operations
Air	Specific activities, comments, and/or details related to the air domain
Cyber	Specific activities, comments, and/or details related to cyber integration
Space	Specific activities, comments, and/or details related to space integration
Multidomain operations	Specific activities, comments, and/or details related to multidomain operations outside space and cyber
Current training	Details about current state of training
Training needs	Details about training needs unique to the AOC
Technology	Technology and software actively used or anticipated
13O	Utilization of the 13O career field

As codes were applied to selections, key points of those selections were further condensed and summarized. Once all the notes were coded, then codes, summaries, and corresponding note selections were systematically extracted to a spreadsheet and compiled as an AOC notes database. This database structure was a simple table containing seven columns, which are shown in Table 5.2, and one row corresponding to each note selection that was coded. Each of the fields in the database could be searched and filtered; this allowed our team to isolate specific points, topics, and terms that came up in discussions across the AOCs.

Table 5.2. Structure of AOC Notes Database

Column	Content
AOC	AOC interviewed
Topic	Code applied to note selection
Summary	Summary of note selection
Comment author	Coder and author of note selection summary
Date	Date that the code and summary were applied
Page	Page number of the note selection
Note selection	Selection of the notes that was coded and summarized

We then further distilled this detailed database by incorporating it into an AOC framework, which summarized the data across the AOCs relevant to the three domains of primary interest (air, space, and cyber) across each of our three primary content areas (training needs, training processes, and training capabilities). Table 5.3 shows the framework for the information we collected across AOCs to facilitate cross-AOC comparison.

Note that there were also sections allowing for general comments pertinent to the three primary content areas (needs, processes, and capabilities) that did not clearly fit into the three domains of primary interest. This summarization helped systematize our consideration of domain elements and facilitated examination of commonalities and differences across the various AOCs that fed into our consideration of current status and the future as perceived by AOC personnel.

Analysis

Our analysis of the consequent AOC-specific data as described above is qualitative, and it highlights critical themes and gaps across the AOCs concerning training needs, processes, and capabilities with an eye to their relevance to JADC2. Much of the assessment of specific AOCs affirmed the general analysis provided in Chapter 3. AOC training is accomplished through academic study, PowerPoint briefings, OJT, and exercises at varying frequencies. Training for the AOC (IQT and MQT) and training at the AOCs (MQT and CT) are quite often focused almost exclusively on preparation for day-to-day operations. Consideration of what the future might look like at the AOC with implementation of JADC2 was not a primary focus.

Table 5.3. Framework for Interview Information Collection

		JADC2 Future	Current Status		
			AOC 1	AOC 2	AOC 3
Domain	General	Needs	Needs	Needs	Needs
		Processes	Processes	Processes	Processes
		Capabilities	Capabilities	Capabilities	Capabilities
	Air	Needs	Needs	Needs	Needs
		Processes	Processes	Processes	Processes
		Capabilities	Capabilities	Capabilities	Capabilities
	Cyber	Needs	Needs	Needs	Needs
		Processes	Processes	Processes	Processes
		Capabilities	Capabilities	Capabilities	Capabilities
	Space	Needs	Needs	Needs	Needs
		Processes	Processes	Processes	Processes
		Capabilities	Capabilities	Capabilities	Capabilities

Thus, it is not surprising that many of our AOC interlocutors reported somewhat limited familiarity with the JADC2 concept,[195] and they presented considerations of what JADC2 might

---

[195] DAF officials, discussions with the authors, January 21, 2021; February 10, 2021; and June 3, 2021.

entail for their given AOC as speculative.[196] Certainly, without knowledge of what exactly implementation might entail, our SMEs were unable to specify how specific jobs or positions might be modified in the future other than in broad brushstrokes. In short, **many AOC personnel simply were not informed well enough about JADC2 to be able to identify relevant training needs specific to JADC2**. The comment below from our interviews, exemplifies this sentiment:

> If you ask most people in the air component staffs, very few people could explain what it is. If you can't explain it, how can you know what you need to do to train for implementation?[197]

This presents a substantial issue, given that any new concept and associated capabilities should respond to the needs of end users (in this case, AOC personnel who may or may not undertake more than one tour of duty at the AOC and hence may entail an ongoing pipeline of trainees and incumbents). However, given that the AOC is doctrinally how the USAF integrates multiple domains, our interlocutors were able to speak to the varying degrees that they executed such integration for the present, and many were aware that JADC2 conceptually would require more such integration. Thus, we also explicitly discussed training needs for other domains.

Some AOCs noted that having sufficient personnel or sufficiently accessible training to enable more training for new concepts would be of benefit.[198] With regard to training needs more generally, several AOCs reported **challenges with manning**, and these indirectly limited opportunities to engage in considerations of what revisions may be needed for a still-in-development concept, such as JADC2.

With regard to training curricula and processes, **integration of multiple domains happens in varying degrees depending on the mission and duties of the AOC**. Geographic AOCs, such as the 603rd, 607th, 609th, and 613th, are more tailored to joint, all-domain operations, whereas global AOCs, such as the 608th, 616th, and 618th, tend to be more confined to a single domain despite the reality that their missions can span multiple AORs. Several of the AOCs are relatively focused on the air domain, and thus are not foreseen to have explicit needs for integration of cyber or space domains and currently do not offer extensive training on their integration.[199] **There is a deficiency in curricula and capabilities for training with space and cyber across the AOCs**, which can be a significant issue given the joint nature of JADC2.

The new-at-the-time 13O career field offers another opportunity to delve into consideration of needs, training process, and capabilities for JADC2, as these officers had more-specific

---

[196] DAF officials, discussions with the authors, January 8, 2021; January 22, 2021; and May 18, 2021.

[197] DAF officials, interview with authors, May 18, 2021.

[198] DAF officials, interviews with authors, January 8, 2021; February 10, 2021; May 26, 2021; and June 3, 2021.

[199] DAF officials, discussions with the authors, January 8, 2021; January 21, 2021; January 22, 2021; February 10, 2021; May 18, 2021; May 26, 2021; and June 3, 2021.

training in multidomain coordination at the operational level. Several of the AOCs had one or more 13O on staff in various roles to help increase expertise with joint considerations. Given these varying roles, at present, **use of the 13O career field is not systematized**, but several SMEs noted that 13Os were already demonstrating utility in various ways, particularly with regard to increasing understanding of nonkinetic effects and with regard to consideration of multiple domains. On the other hand, the lack of systematization could also be seen to reflect some of the uncertainty regarding implementation of JADC2 at the AOC. The comments below illustrate these perceptions:

> 13O is going to be essential to the integration of the different domains and services.[200]

> It seems like currently 13O is useful and we find a place where we can use them, but there is not a specific role for them at the AOC.[201]

> There is some resistance to the new way of development for 13O and how that would affect how the regular air force is developing. Also, a lack of knowledge on what a 13O is.[202]

With regard to AOC capabilities and training software, many interlocutors made it clear that they anticipated that mechanisms for future integration would be necessary. ABMS is characterized as being one such mechanism for eventual integration, with KRADOS serving this purpose in the interim. At the time of our interviews, at least six AOCs had some exposure to KRADOS or other Kessel Run apps. However, **relatively few AOC personnel had substantial experience with the developmental applications intended to support JADC2**. In some cases, this is because the systems they used and their missions were quite different from a more "typical" warfighting AOC (e.g., 608th), so KRADOS might have less applicability. In other cases, this was simply because KRADOS and certainly ABMS are very much in development.

Currently, particularly for space and cyber, there are **challenges with integrating new software (potentially for training) in the day-to-day operations**. Many interlocutors implied that they had relatively little need for technical capabilities supporting multidomain integration of space and cyber, because the operational integration of space and cyber was presently limited.[203] Some interlocutors mentioned complexities regarding authorities, whereas others noted challenges with differing classification levels.[204] Several commented on the difficulties in understanding the nature of effects in these domains.

---

[200] DAF officials, interview with authors, April 19, 2021.

[201] DAF officials, interview with authors, May 26, 2021.

[202] DAF officials, interview with authors, January 28, 2021.

[203] DAF officials, discussions with the authors, January 8, 2021; February 10, 2021; February 16, 2021; May 18, 2021; May 26, 2021; and June 3, 2021.

[204] See also Priebe et al., 2020.

How LVC Can Support JADC2 Training

Given the intent of JADC2 and the capabilities that LVC training provides, both detailed in previous chapters, we find that LVC can support training for JADC2 in general, and in this section, we summarize why this is so. We first summarize how general characteristics of LVC (and its independent components) align with JADC2-related training needs itemized in Chapter 2, and thus confirm that LVC can be beneficial. Then, given that we have discussed ways in which LVC can support specific aspects of JADC2 throughout the report, we present benefits in the form of a high-level road map for consideration as JADC2 matures. Frameworks detailed in previous chapters are summarized in terms of how LVC can support JADC2 training. As discussed in Chapter 2, the general intent of JADC2 is to facilitate networked C2. LVC, as an overall construct, fundamentally involves the networking of users involved in individual or collective training, whether they use live or virtual training capabilities and whether they integrate with computer-based systems or entities. Thus, as many interview subjects suggested, LVC capabilities do not just enhance training for JADC2; they are *necessary* for training JADC2, given the anticipated nature of the emerging operational concept.

As discussed in Chapter 4, LVC (considering the overall construct as well as the value of individual components) provides the ability to do the following:

1. Integrate and/or network multiple users, possibly at different locations.
2. Train on rare or inaccessible events like near-peer competition. LVC may have a particularly important role to play with simulating Red air.[205] LVC can include constructive (computer-based) entities that interface with live aggressor pilots. Additionally, LVC provides an excellent framework for EW training using off-board, off-range EW hardware in the loop or onboard EW simulations carried in training pods.
3. Practice particularly challenging or risky scenarios, such as faster decisionmaking and/or warfare with degraded communications and geographic positioning system denial.
4. Test and practice integration and collaboration across organizations, whether these organizations be different MAJCOMs, services, or international partners.
5. Practice changes in delegation of authority, such as increased distribution (reduced centralization).
6. Represent desired capabilities, environments, and/or scenarios via virtual content.
7. Represent adversaries (Red air) for relatively little cost.

Table 5.4 consolidates the JADC2 requirements and various training requirements outlined in Chapter 2 and maps the consequent training needs to these LVC benefits. LVC clearly provides benefit to training for JADC2, especially with regard to training resilient, distributed, and decentralized C2. It is generally less useful in responding to the need for dynamic tasking, assessment, and analysis of large datasets and operationally complex environments. It can certainly be helpful in training for these issues, but this is not necessarily where it provides unique training value. For example, the virtual component of LVC, in particular, can be helpful

---

[205] *Red air* denotes adversaries.

with simulating operationally complex environments and with presenting large amounts of data, but LVC as an overall construct (including linked LVC training) for integrating multiple concurrent users is less critical for such needs.

Table 5.4. Alignment of JADC2 Training Requirements and LVC Capabilities

Training Need	Applicable LVC Benefit
Resilient, distributed, and decentralized C2	1, 2, 3, 5
C2 at a faster pace	1, 3
Dynamic tasking	
Data assessment and analysis	6[a]
Understanding and using effects from multiple domains and using a multidomain COP	1, 4
Operationally complex environments	6
Collaboration and operation across AOCs	1
Using and combating AI/ML and autonomous systems	6, 7

[a] Certain virtual technologies, detailed in Chapter 3, can be helpful with human-computer interaction and access to data.

Throughout this work, we have noted training needs that LVC can address most effectively. We have also presented frameworks for illustrating how LVC may be valuable in the future. Table 5.5 summarizes these frameworks and opportunities for leveraging LVC as JADC2 and related concepts and capabilities mature.

Table 5.5. Opportunities for Leveraging LVC

Framework for Assessing JADC2	LVC Relevance
Potential changes in ATO process (Chapter 2, Tables 2.1 and 2.2, Figures 2.2 and E.1)	• Useful in most stages of the ATO cycle • Reduces unnecessary white-carding with ATO training • Facilitates higher fidelity and more-complex in-house training at AOCs
Potential changes in AOC structure (Chapter 3, Figure 3.4)	• Prepares for and enables distributed AOC structure, allowing integration of multiple C2 nodes (potentially among AOCs and tactical operators) • Enables training for cloud-based AC structure • Allows integration with more-extensive simulation capabilities not available at all AOCs
Increased use of distributed training exercises (Chapter 3, Figure 3.3)	• Enables increased accessibility and participation • Reduces unnecessary white-carding, allowing more AOCs to garner training benefits from exercises rather than just support exercises
Development of distributed training architectures (Chapter 4, Figure 4.4 and Table 4.3)	• Provides an integral and necessary keystone for distributed training • Facilitates integration of AOC staff with other tactical nodes during training exercises • Allows testing of existing and new distributed training federations and capabilities

Framework for Assessing JADC2	LVC Relevance
Development of a common IT architecture (Chapter 4, Figure 4.3)	• Provides testing and training capabilities, including space and cyber systems • Aligns the software acquisitions process for test, training, and AOC operational systems

As Table 5.5 illustrates, there are multiple perspectives to and aspects of JADC2 under development that could provide insertion points for using LVC. A key issue for developers and policymakers is LVC insertion *while* these aspects (AOCs, ATOs, training exercises, etc.) evolve, not after. As JADC2 advances more-distributed operations that affect ATOs, AOCs, training exercises, and software systems, LVC will not just be beneficial, but necessary, and it plays an important role in the efficient development of relevant concepts.

Conclusion

Often, as new concepts and capabilities emerge, the end user is not able to provide input as much and as early in the development cycle as needed. This results in challenges in development, in that the needs of the end user are not adequately considered, and the final product may be less relevant to their needs. Thus, especially with training, it is critical to aggregate input from the end user (the training audience) and to tie processes and capabilities to actual underlying needs. Furthermore, it is important not just to assess the value of new training capabilities but to understand how they could and should be implemented, given the current approaches to training. To understand more thoroughly how LVC can help support USAF training for JADC2 and what is needed across AOCs, we provided two final analyses. First, we composed and analyzed a matrix concerning AOC needs, processes, and capabilities. Second, we aggregated analysis from previous chapters to yield a basic road map for using LVC to train AOCs in support of JADC2.

The most glaring finding when evaluating trends across the AOCs was the lack of understanding of what JADC2 will entail and the implications of this new concept to AOC operations. This in turn can impede AOC personnel in voicing training needs. Yet, as noted earlier, when developing new capabilities or new warfighting concepts, both of which require joint interoperability and collaboration, understanding user needs is especially critical.

Additional primary findings from this analysis are highlighted as follows:

- **Current C2 operators at the AOC have limited familiarity with JADC2.** In part, this is because the concept is in development; however, given that these are the personnel who will implement the concept in the USAF, their integration and feedback would be valuable early in the process.
- **There is a need for better understanding of joint operations.** C2 operators at the AOCs vary in their ability to understand and integrate multiple domains. Even for space and cyber, integration is limited, accomplished via deliberate (manual) coordination rather than seamless simulation. Training in multiple domains is similarly limited.

- In the AOC, **manning levels may not be sufficient** to allow for training for dramatically different ways of engaging in operations, because day-to-day operations may take most of AOC personnel's time.
- **The use of LVC for training can help the USAF align training approaches and capabilities with user needs** arising specifically from JADC2.
  - LVC can help support JADC2 training and may be especially helpful with supporting resilient, distributed, and decentralized C2.
- **There are distinct opportunities for leveraging LVC** more extensively, and these relate to ATOs, AOC structure, training exercises, and distributed training federations and architectures.

Chapter 6. Discussion, Findings, and Recommendations

As the nature of warfare changes, warfighting concepts adapt, and so too must training. DoD is developing JADC2 as the latest warfighting concept. It represents a significant change in the way DoD fights, with an effort to link every sensor to every shooter, regardless of domain. Given this paradigm shift, training processes and capabilities must adapt as the concept matures, with continual input from the user. Especially in the USAF, a key component of training and the OTTI is LVC. Thus, this study reflects a systematic and thorough analysis of how LVC might support JADC2.

We address the following overarching questions:

- What are the primary training needs with respect to anticipated requirements for JADC2 across AOCs?
- What are the processes and curricula for CT at AOCs?
- Which LVC capabilities that are available or under development could help support training related to JADC2?

To understand relevant training needs, we provide a continuum of analyses that maps from anticipated characteristics of warfare to relevant types of skills (for C2). With a focus on AOC personnel and tier 3 and tier 4 training, and in an effort to itemize training needs relevant to JADC2, we evaluate relevant missions, AOC-specific training requirements, doctrinal implications for training, and instructional programs for C2, parsing the training requirements necessary to support JADC2. With an understanding of the relevant training needs, we then evaluate the current process for setting training requirements, including an assessment of various joint and USAF task lists that could potentially help characterize training needs and identify where LVC might be most useful. Because the ATO cycle is a primary activity in AOCs and thus contextualizes primary training needs, we present a new framework for analyzing ATOs, how they may shift as JADC2 develops, and how LVC can support this shift.

With a set of training requirements as a foundation, we then study the training processes at AOCs. This includes a review of IQT, MQT, and especially CT. As part of CT, we study the training exercise planning process and how LVC would factor in this process most effectively. We also analyze sources of variation in training among different types of AOCs. Finally, we look at the current and potential structure of AOCs, illustrating how this structure may change and how it may facilitate the use of LVC.

We then review the state of the art with respect to LVC capabilities that could support JADC2. First, we review USAF documentation to assess the perceived value of LVC and plans for future development. As a baseline for improving consistent communication across the JADC2 community with respect to IT systems, we develop a new context map for IT components related to JADC2. We review actual ongoing programs (including an in-depth

90

analysis of Block 20 and ABMS) and development efforts inside and outside the USAF, and we map the current and emerging technology to JADC2 requirements. Recognizing that there is minimal ongoing effort to support training systems with integration to JADC2-related software, we review all existing and developmental distributed training systems and architectures to identify opportunities to leverage available systems. Finally, in response to the indicated deficiencies with training for space and cyber in the AOCs, we review current and potential challenges with using LVC for space and cyber training.

With a foundational analysis of needs, processes, and capabilities, we then summarize how the USAF can leverage LVC to train for JADC2 most effectively. This involves systematically assessing each AOC with respect to unique training needs, training curricula, and capabilities for JADC2. We then map the JADC2 training requirements to the most salient benefits of LVC to determine how LVC may be most beneficial in general. When combined with frameworks for evaluating potential changes in AOCs, ATOs, and technology, this yields a basic road map of LVC-related opportunities that the USAF can consider as JADC2 matures.

Discussion

Throughout this work, a series of central and relatively broad themes emerged. These themes are discussed in this section, followed by a series of key overarching findings, and then recommendations for facilitating effective training for JADC2.

A recurrent theme in many of our discussions with Air Force and DoD officials is that **there can be confusion and a lack of clarity as to who is doing what with respect to JADC2 efforts and what JADC2 will entail**. Coordination among JADC2 stakeholders will likely be critical for its success. For example, a senior leader involved in the Air Force's JADC2 activities noted that many offices involved in ABMS would provide different descriptions of what ABMS is and what it entails. The same official noted that a flat, distributed management structure may not be most appropriate for a complex program meant to address a problem that is not sharply defined.[206]

JADC2 activities beyond the Air Force and across the other services and Joint Staff similarly demonstrate a lack of integration and misunderstandings about the roles, responsibilities, and purposes behind different JADC2-related efforts. One official noted that the lack of coordination among DoD and the services created difficulties for allied air forces that are interested in aligning their activities with JADC2 as it develops.[207] One potential issue standing in the way of

---

[206] DAF official, interview with authors, March 2021.

[207] DAF official, interview with authors, March 4, 2021.

closer coordination among the services is a lack of incentive to provide resources in support of each other's JADC2 development activities.[208]

The vision of JADC2 to enable information flow across domains entails new sets of interactions and tools—for example, the use of AI/ML in decisionmaking, the potential reconfiguration of C2 structures, and the potential to task assets from other domains—that are unfamiliar to the cultures of the services, according to a Marine Corps official.[209] Multiple DAF officials noted that AOC officials generally lack familiarity with the capabilities that can potentially be brought to bear from other domains, such as cyber, and that practice will be required to familiarize them with those effects and tasking cycles for other domains.[210] This underlines the need for a common understanding of what JADC2 is across units within the DAF and the across the services.

Another common theme, in addition to the challenges of consistent and continual communication, is potential cultural resistance to substantial changes. **Integration of multiple domains poses a cultural challenge for JADC2 at the AOCs.** At many AOCs, there is limited day-to-day integration of cyber and space domains; the primary area of concentration is the air domain.[211] Integration of other domains, such as land and sea, primarily takes place through LNOs,[212] and in some cases, actual incorporation of effects in other domains requires cumbersome navigation of authorities' processes.[213] This would not necessarily pose a significant challenge to incorporating multiple domains if the majority of Air Force officers billeted at AOCs were very familiar with effects and planning in all domains, but this is not necessarily the case. Air Force efforts to conceptualize multidomain operations at the AOC suggest that familiarity with multiple domains is not truly common, and our AOC interlocutors shared that additional expertise would be quite helpful to incorporate them. Specific joint education requirements are certainly incorporated in the DAF as part of Intermediate Developmental Education (IDE) and Senior Developmental Education. IDE is typically attended by officers with the rank of major, meaning officers are relatively senior when they receive this exposure.[214] Finally, Gallei explicitly notes critical capability gaps that the Air Force was attempting to alleviate through the development of the 13O career field include expertise in joint

---

[208] Army officials, interview with authors, June 8, 2021; Theresa Hitchens, "Combatant Commands Worry About Service JADC2 Stovepipes," *Breaking Defense*, August 31, 2021e.

[209] Marine Corps official, interview with authors, August 24, 2021.

[210] DAF official, interview with authors, August 27, 2021.

[211] DAF officials, interviews with authors, various dates; see also Priebe et al., 2020.

[212] DAF officials, interviews with authors, various dates; see also Priebe et al., 2020.

[213] Priebe et al., 2020.

[214] The content should focus on joint warfighting in the context of operational to strategic levels, theater strategy, operational art in all domains, and joint leader development (Chairman of the Joint Chiefs of Staff Instruction 1800.01F, *Officer Professional Military Education Policy*, Joint Chiefs of Staff, May 15, 2020).

and multidomain operations planning.[215] Although the Air Force is now phasing out this career field, the gap remains, and the intent is to fill it by emphasizing multidomain competencies more widely across the force.[216]

The balance between centralization and decentralization poses a cultural challenge as well, when considering the incorporation of multiple domains at the level of operational C2 in the USAF. Mills and colleagues highlighted how the Air Force has let the operational art of providing support to more-agile expeditionary concepts atrophy during the recent history of rapid deployments.[217] However, the AOC represents centralized C2 control, which potentially poses a challenge to the decentralized and distributed C2 that may be necessary in the future. Historically, the AOC came into its own in the first Gulf War and was ultimately institutionalized into a weapon system with the intent to increase standardization and to centralize control of airpower and was the result of years of effort to do so.[218] Others note the extent to which such a centralized C2 construct is dependent on undisturbed communications, which are very likely to be challenged in conflicts with peer or near-peer adversaries.[219] Mulgund (2021) speaks to the historical impetus for centralized command and the enduring tension between centralization and decentralization, and he also describes some of the Air Force's current efforts to alleviate these challenges.[220] However, the decades-long push for, and success of, centralized C2 at the AOC speaks more generally to a lack of familiarity in the Air Force with some of the skills that will be needed to obviate the threats represented by contestation of communications. To develop the skills—and trust—necessary to implement such practices with confidence, practice and training will be necessary, not just at the AOC but also with operators at the tactical edge.

Implementation of technology innovation can be stymied if culture is not considered. ABMS is expected to be the technical backbone of JADC2. The joint force operators and strategic decisionmakers' ability to operate ABMS and capitalize on capabilities will be crucial to JADC2 employment. Although the Air Force is known for its "worship at the altar of

---

[215] Gallei, 2020.

[216] "Air Force to Phase Out 13O Career Field, Strengthen All Airmen Joint Capabilities," U.S. Air Force, February 17, 2022.

[217] Patrick Mills, James A. Leftwich, John G. Drew, Daniel P. Felten, Josh Girardini, John P. Godges, Michael J. Lostumbo, Anu Narayanan, Kristin Van Abel, Jonathan William Welburn, and Anna Jean Wirth, *Building Agile Combat Support Competencies to Enable Evolving Adaptive Basing Concepts*, RAND Corporation, RR-4200-AF, 2020.

[218] Joseph H. Justice III, "Airpower Command and Control: Evolution of the Air and Space Operations Center as a Weapon System," U.S. Army, March 19, 2004.

[219] Russell Cook, *The Next Step: A Study on Resilience in Command and Control*, U.S. Air Force, June 1, 2015; Lingel et al., 2020; Priebe et al., 2020.

[220] Mulgund, 2021.

technology," technology alone is not sufficient, as business has shown again and again.[221] Many executives and businesses consider that approximately one in three planned change initiatives meets with success.[222] Notably, the examination of technology adoption in organizations has generated its own extensive literature because it represents a persistent problem, including in the military.[223] Two relatively recent *meta-analyses* (quantitative aggregations of many studies) looked in particular at the technology acceptance model and highlight the importance of user perceptions, particularly perceptions of the technology's usefulness and perceived attitudes of the importance to others, in technology implementation.[224] This serves to highlight the importance of shared beliefs and perceptions for whether technology adaptation is appropriate behavior. As described, ABMS and the substantial changes to the AOC contemplated under JADC2 would represent changes to the technical core of C2 in the Air Force. Such changes would potentially have strong influence on the way that the work is done—that is, the essential products and services of the business (in this case, the AOC). As noted by Ryan, Harrison, and Schkade (2002), radical changes of this form have the greatest potential to cause social subsystem disruption.[225] They found that even in cases in which technological change is likely to be quite disruptive and organizations were focused strategically on technology (as the Air Force is), their surveyed executives were likely to give relatively scant consideration to change management efforts to alleviate social subsystem disruption. They further noted that organizations ignore these costs at their peril.

---

[221] Carl H. Builder, *The Masks of War: American Military Styles in Strategy and Analysis*, Johns Hopkins University Press, 1989, p. 19.

[222] Jeroen Stouten, Denise M. Rousseau, and David de Cremer, "Successful Organizational Change: Integrating the Management Practice and Scholarly Literatures," *Academy of Management Annals*, Vol. 12, No. 2, 2018.

[223] Harrison, 2021.

[224] This model suggests that technology adaptation is a function of perceived usefulness of technology and perceived ability to use the technology, which combine to form an intention to use the technology (see William R. King and Jun He, "A Meta-Analysis of the Technology Acceptance Model, *Information & Management*, Vol. 43, No. 6, 2006). King and He noted that perceived technological usefulness was the strongest predictor of adaptation in the model. Schepers and Wetzels (2007) included an examination of subjective norms (i.e., perceived attitudes of the importance to others and perceptions of what behaviors may be normative) in the Technology Acceptance Model and found that norms were related to both perceived usefulness of technology and actual intention to use the technology, suggesting the influence of the social context in technology adaptation (Jeroen Schepers and Martin Wetzels, "A Meta-Analysis of the Technology Acceptance Model: Investigating Subjective Norm and Moderation Effects," *Information & Management*, Vol. 44, No. 1, 2007).

[225] Sherry D. Ryan, David A. Harrison, and Lawrence L. Schkade, "Information-Technology Investment Decisions: When Do Costs and Benefits in the Social Subsystem Matter?" *Journal of Management Information Systems*, Vol. 19, No. 2, 2002.

Primary Findings

Although specific findings are discussed at the end of each chapter, primary overarching findings are summarized as follows, grouped in terms of relevance to training needs, processes and curricula, and capabilities.

JADC2 and Training Needs

The intent of the JADC2 concept and supporting capabilities risks being unclear across echelons. Conceptualizations of C2, in particular, have significant, if currently unclear, implications for the tactical level. Uncertainty among potential end users applies not only to the overarching JADC2 concept but also to software systems. The role of ABMS relative to other systems risks being unclear, given other existing and planned systems, particularly Kessel Run's effort with the new AOC weapon system.

Balancing centralized coordination with decentralized needs will be critical to effective training development. As noted, JADC2 simultaneously incentivizes both the centralization and distribution of C2, and various USAF conceptions of the future AOC diverge along this spectrum. Two relatively consistent themes emerge from the ongoing debate about the future of the AOC. The first is a distribution of at least some of the AOC functions even if control remains centralized. The second is greater connectivity and collaboration among the AOC, tactical elements, and key enablers via a resilient, cloud-based network. Considerations also include further development of the concept of mission command and its application to the USAF. Development of trust and the requisite skill sets is essential, and tactical commanders will need to understand that operational and higher-level commanders trust them to accept prudent risk and to execute actions under conditions when communication is contested. The coordination processes will require time to develop, and the operators will require time to learn. Discussion of the evolution of mission command highlighted the utility of exercises to help develop practical methods and systems of execution and overcome some of the potential cultural issues described above.

As JADC2 develops, it is essential to consider adaptations of the training process to support it. Actual training needs must derive from both strategic needs as well as the needs of the operators who will execute these imperatives. Given the variation across AOCs in the status quo, anticipated differences in the impact of JADC2 across AOCs, and the as-yet-unclear differences in organizational structure of AOCs, it is not yet clear whether all AOCs will ultimately need the same access to LVC and software capabilities. However, the need for LVC and additional capabilities to facilitate practice will be acute for some, and the USAF should be prepared to provide them. Although the JADC2 concept is still developing, it is not too early to consider training issues, and training exercises may be used to help collect data to consider implementation of the concept itself. Certain aspects of the concept are converging, and some needs are clear, regardless of their ultimate specific implementation. The time to begin consideration of training needs as well as infrastructure is now, not after developmental silos have eroded the possibilities for true interoperability. This impetus is quite clear both from prior historical program efforts,[226] as well as the current work, which shows indication of similar issues. The nature of JADC2, reliant as it is on intense communication and coordination across domains, requires greater attention to alignment from the beginning.

Training Processes and Curricula

IQT is a useful lever to build necessary JADC2 expertise and will continue to provide a mechanism for centralized coordination. Given the distinct functional and geographic missions of different AOCs, we observe much more variation when it comes to local MQT and CT programs than we do for IQT, which is an important touchpoint for standardization. Some of this variation reflects a purposeful balance between centralized coordination and decentralized training needs, but this variation also stems from relative gaps in resources and training opportunities from one AOC to the next. Although implementation of JADC2 may arise organically as various AOCs tackle the concept over time, given the need for coordination inherent in the concept itself, it may behoove the USAF to ensure a clear understanding of the concept and what the USAF considers essential elements through a centralized mechanism, such as IQT. However, given the limitations of IQT in terms of scope, it may not be sufficient, and other options should be considered.

In general, **AOC personnel tend to support training exercises but are less frequently involved as the targeted training audience**. As described, however, implementation of JADC2 has the potential to greatly affect their work. Therefore, they are a key training audience and will be key users of any innovative technology. Providing the resources to fully experience the implication of JADC2 via LVC and enabling the AOC to practice the entire ATO cycle fully, without white-carding, would be of benefit.

Training Capabilities

LVC can potentially support training for JADC2, and centralized LVC resources may be key to executing the complex needs of future training. As the AOCs move toward some of the implementation options considered, even those that currently have access to resources, such as training centers that provide LVC capabilities that enable execution of more-complex training, may ultimately lose access to such resources as their structure becomes more decentralized and less infrastructure-heavy. Thus, centralized and widely available LVC-capable training resources may become even more valuable as we see such trends as greater distribution of AOC functions and the incorporation of a cloud-based architecture that is less reliant on fixed infrastructure to manage key AOC processes. Each of these evolutions will alter the AOC training paradigm in a

---

[226] Harrison, 2021.

way that increases the need for LVC training capabilities. Many AOCs do not have the manning or, in some cases, capabilities to create the requisite training: As with current IQT, centralized development of resources for AOCs to use will be essential. This has the added benefit for providing an inherent mechanism for coordination.

Given the operational and technical complexity of JADC2, as well as its inherently joint nature, there is a risk of siloed development. This can result in acquisition inefficiencies, but more importantly, it can result in operational failure if there is a substantial lack of coordination among services. Given the available and developing systems that operationalize training, this risk is particularly poignant in the training arena. Such risks are certainly not new in the acquisition community, and there are potential difficulties with implementation that touch perennial challenges, such as interoperability and incentivized coordination across services. Relevant software systems like C2IMERA are intended to address C2 needs, but different software systems, developed by different services, are not necessarily coordinated. Furthermore, it is not clear that training capabilities are being considered or developed alongside new AOC weapon systems or components of ABMS.

There are a variety of ways in which LVC can support training for JADC2:

- Many effects are white-carded at AOC exercises (e.g., disrupted C2), including CCMD exercises. Using LVC could support a larger number of, and increased realism of, training repetitions for dealing with effects that will stress C2 functions.
- Understanding and using a multidomain COP will be important for AOC functions and training, but this is currently rare. LVC could be useful for populating a COP for training.
- Operators will need to build trust and experience with AI/ML tools adopted for JADC2 and AOC functions. Rigorous testing of these risky AI/ML tools must be undertaken using the entire tool chain of JADC2. LVC can provide testing, verification, and validation as well as training opportunities and simulated data to feed into AI/ML tools.
- There can be challenges with providing integrated training that reaches across training tiers, involving CCMDs as well as multiple services concurrently. Currently, CCMDs address tiers 1 and 2, and services address tiers 3 and 4. Yet, JADC2 will necessarily involve multitier operations across all tiers concurrently. LVC could support integrated training across training tiers, mending this disconnect, especially with large-scale training exercises.

Recommendations

Recommendations are summarized as follows, in alignment with the findings discussed above. The recommendations involve a few key stakeholders. As the primary lead for JADC2 efforts across DoD, the JADC2 CFT can help coordinate relevant information and education. In the joint community, JS J6 is the JADC2 CFT lead, and JS J7 oversees joint training. In the USAF, AF/A3T provides oversight for training, and the 505th Combat Training Group focuses on executing IQT as well as other AOC-related training, such as training for the 13O career field.

AFAMS houses technical expertise in the modeling and simulation domain but with a focus on training capabilities.

JADC2 and Training Needs

1. **The JADC2 CFT should take the lead in distributing a well-coordinated and regularly updated portfolio of material concerning JADC2 goals, plans, and capabilities.** This effort should target all services and multiple echelons, including AOC staff. In general, the JADC2 strategy is handed down from senior leadership, but it should incorporate feedback and input directly form AOC users.

    a. Establishing a common language with respect to JADC2 software, IT, and distributed training capabilities could help facilitate collaboration among organizations.
    b. AF/A3T can help facilitate consistent communication in the USAF training community.

2. **The JADC2 CFT should systematically define and communicate training goals for JADC2,** which will in turn facilitate appropriate capability development. To incorporate JADC2 effectively, training goals must systematically be defined before training is executed. Under JADC2, AOC personnel may require greater joint context and joint interactions in operational and tactical (tiers 3 and 4) C2 training.[227] However, the current training requirements process is not well designed to specify how JADC2 requirements might inform tier 3 and 4 training for AOCs. Moreover, the granularity of the tasks used as the basis for CT is not appropriate for specifying a role for LVC. The current requirements process does not support an interpretation of what capabilities may be necessary. It is unlikely that appropriate capabilities will arise organically through the process without directed effort.

    a. The DAF and JS J6 should add new tasks and new detail for existing tasks to the Universal Joint Task List (UJTL) and the Air Force Universal Task List (AFUTL). This will provide an updated mechanism for defining training goals and planning training exercises.

3. **In collaboration with AF/A3T, the 505th Combat Training Group should leverage IQT as a mechanism for centralized coordination of C2 (and ultimately, JADC2) training across AOCs.** Although IQT alone is likely insufficient for building necessary JADC2 expertise, it does provide one mechanism for coordination across AOCs.

    a. As another mechanism for centralized coordination, the DAF and AF/A3T should continue development and deployment of the 13O career field skill set now that the career field is being sunset.

Training Processes and Curricula

4. **With oversight from AF/A3T, individual AOCs should focus on CT that involves the complete AOC staff and not just individual sections or units.** This will likely require improved manning.

---

[227] Joint Staff officials, interview with authors, April 19, 2021.

5. **The 505th Combat Training Group, as part of IQT, and each AOC, as part of CT, should incorporate scenarios that test cultural norms into training curricula**, preparing leadership at all echelons for potential changes in the delegation of authority and contested C2 that is different from the traditional paradigm of centralized OPCON at the AOC.

6. In accordance with the discussion in Chapter 5, **AF/A3T should leverage LVC for AOC C2 training during distributed training exercises**, with AOC staff participating in active roles and not just support roles. With oversight of and technical support for joint training, JS J7 could play a supporting role, especially regarding integration with other services.

7. **With oversight from AF/A3T, all aspects of training (IQT, MQT, and CT) should involve increased time reviewing tactical and operational C2 levels of other domains' tasking process and capabilities.**

   a. Space and cyber ATO processes are relatively long and siloed, and AOCs will need training capabilities to provide experience with space and cyber effects.

Training Capabilities

8. **The JADC2 CFT and JS J7 should leverage existing and developing distributed training systems for JADC2 and ensure ABMS integrates with LVC training capabilities.** Current efforts to develop or integrate with training capabilities in support of JADC2 are minimal. However, as illustrated in Table 4.3, there are opportunities to use, integrate with, or at least learn from existing systems without unnecessary duplicative development.

9. **AF/A3T should distribute the IT context map in Figure 4.3** across the JADC2 and USAF training communities to help foster a common dialogue about fundamental IT components for JADC2 and how they are related.

10. **AF/A3T should guide increased use of LVC in the capacities outlined in Table 5.4.** Although LVC can add value to training in general, there are specific areas in which LVC use should be considered as organizations, systems, or processes evolve to support JADC2. These include changes in the ATO process, changes in the AOC structure, increased use of distributed training, and development of a common IT architecture.

11. **With oversight from AF/A3T, a single organization—perhaps AFAMS or the 505th—should be involved in the process to plan large training exercises and should focus on integrating LVC capabilities consistently.** Training exercises are a natural insertion point for current and new LVC capabilities in support of JADC2. Consequently, there needs to be a central USAF technology advisor tracking the use of LVC capabilities across AOCs and various training exercises. Having a central organization involved in this process, and not just the training planners and audience, will help in maintaining consistent deployment and use of LVC capabilities.

12. **To facilitate integration of multidomain training, AF/A3T should work with CCMDs, combat support agencies, other services, and MAJCOMs** to enhance AOC training with space and cyber effects. As with AOCs in general, space and cyber staff should participate as part of the training audience, not just as training support. This would require providing AOCs with necessary capabilities and manning to train with space and cyber effects. There will likely be cultural issues with regard to incorporating other domains in tier 3 and tier 4 training at the AOCs. This lack of general awareness naturally

carries through to a lack of specific awareness with regard to other domains' tasking process and capabilities. In particular, space and cyber ATO processes are comparatively long and siloed.[228]

Future Work

In addition to providing substantive findings and recommendations for supporting JADC2 with LVC, we have fleshed out areas that warrant future work. Primarily, there is an opportunity for services and allies to coordinate more effectively, from a technical perspective, in preparing for JADC2 training. As noted in Chapter 2, other services have programs dedicated to JADC2, and the Air Force would benefit from an in-depth review of which organizations (within each service) are involved in development efforts, what capabilities are being developed, what provisions there are for anticipated training, and how the Air Force can integrate more effectively with respect to organizational and R&D efforts.

Related to this effort, additional work is needed with detailed technical assessment of the various current and developmental distributed training systems. This should include a systematic analysis of each system's scope, intent, software and architecture structure, and underlying models. This in turn could yield opportunities for improved integration within and across services.

Within the Air Force, there is a need to assess the mechanisms for, and degree of coordination with regard to training simulator and simulation acquisition and to identify any gaps in capabilities or risks of duplicated effort. Just as there is a need to foster interoperability and collaboration across services in support of JADC2, there is a comparable need to do the same across MAJCOMs and system program offices (SPOs) in the Air Force and thus avoid potential siloed development and use. There remain both technical and organizational challenges with acquisition interoperability and coordination, and there may be opportunities for improved coordination among the various MAJCOMs and SPOs. Each MAJCOM can have unique missions and mission design series and thus unique training needs. In addition, each MAJCOM and SPO can evolve over time with somewhat independent organizational structures and policies.[229] Thus, technology development and deployment risk being siloed. In this context—as with training AOCs—the Air Force must balance distinct decentralized needs and structures with centralized coordination, which can help save money, increase efficiency, and distribute novel training capabilities. Ultimately, this can help improve warfighter readiness.

---

[228] See also Priebe et al., 2020.

[229] A *mission design series* essentially represents a particular system or version of that system (e.g., F-22).

Appendix A. Instructional Programs for C2 Officers

Table A.1 lists and describes educational programs for C2 officer training programs as coded in the CIP taxonomy, which was developed by the U.S. Department of Education's National Center for Education Statistics. The CIP Code is the instructional program code assigned to each program based on the CIP taxonomy. O*NET provides a crosswalk between these programs and various Air Force jobs.

Table A.1. Instructional Programs for Command and Control Center Officers

CIP Code	Program Name	Program Description
29.0204	Command & Control (C3, C4I [command, control, communications, computers, and intelligence]) Systems and Operations	A program that focuses on the theory, technology, and operational use of information and decision systems in support of battlefield, theater, and global strategic operations. Includes instruction in applied mathematics and statistics, computer systems, real-time analysis and decision systems, surveillance and navigation systems, information and communications technology, information security, situational awareness, system integration, joint operations, and applications to specific command problems and services.
29.0205	Information Operations/Joint Information Operations	A program that focuses on the strategic and operational use of information relative to the support of military and strategic policy and objectives. Includes instruction in IT, decision theory and applications, military operations, C2 technology, network operations, network systems integration, computer network defense, space communications technology, and applications to specific military operational tasks.
29.0206	Information/Psychological Warfare and Military Media Relations	A program that focuses on the support of military and strategic operations and policy via the use of information as a tool of statecraft and warfighting. Includes instruction in information technology and systems; information security; C2; satellite communications; global information dissemination; communications and media management; intelligence; psychological warfare; strategic planning; security policy and doctrine; and applications to specific operations, services, and scenarios.
29.0207	Cyber/Electronic Operations and Warfare	A program that focuses on the technological and operation aspects of information warfare, including cyberattack and cyber defense. Includes instruction in computer and network security, cryptography, computer forensics, systems security engineering, software applications, threat and vulnerability assessment, wireless networks and satellite communications, tactical and strategic planning, legal and ethical issues, and cyber warfare systems development and acquisition.
29.0299	Intelligence, Command Control and Information Operations, Other	Any instructional program in intelligence, command control, and information operations not listed above.
29.0405	Joint Command/Task Force (C3, C4I) Systems	A program that focuses on the principles, technology, and operational use of C2 (C3, C4I) systems as applied to joint and combined military operations involving unified commands. Includes instruction in information technology, communications systems, network systems and architecture, systems engineering, C3 and C4I doctrine and policy, C3 and C4I systems management, intelligence, operational and strategic planning, interagency operations, operational security, and deception.
29.0406	Military Information Systems Technology	A program that focuses on the principles, design, and application of computer and networking technology to the military environment. Includes instruction in planning; program development; graphical user interfaces; rapid prototyping; program construction; data types, operations; control flow; arrays; records; file input/output; database access; event-driven object oriented programming structures; and enabling global-networked communications, including databases, systems analysis and design, decision support systems, and network security.

102

Appendix B. Main Stakeholders for JADC2

The JS J6 is taking the lead on coordinating JADC2 efforts across the services.[230] The JADC2 CFT includes general/flag officer and civilian equivalent representatives from the services, the Office of the Secretary of Defense (OSD), the Joint Staff, CCMDs, other government agencies, and some allied states. The CFT is tasked with supporting the Joint Requirements Oversight Council in making determinations on requirements, identifying capability gaps, and generally supporting the integration of service efforts but does not have decisionmaking authority.[231]

Although the whole of DoD is involved in efforts to implement JADC2, various services and offices have more-specific AORs. The Air Force is developing the ABMS as its primary contribution to JADC2.[232] Within the Air Force, the ABMS CFT in Air Force Futures is providing strategic direction to the Air Force's JADC2 efforts.

Within the Air Force, concept and technical development is spread across multiple organizations. The DAF Rapid Capabilities Office is managing the acquisition portion of the ABMS program and is the technical lead. The Chief Architect's Office[233] under the Assistant Secretary of the Air Force for Acquisition, Technology, and Logistics is responsible for the ABMS demonstrations, which bring together the services and industry to experiment with capabilities for ABMS.[234] Future ABMS exercises are intended to place a heavier emphasis on CCMD participation in experimenting with JADC2 capabilities, including in virtual environments.[235]

Other organizations play important roles for developing, testing, and implementing aspects of JADC2. The 505th Combat Training Group supports training, experimentation, and tactics development for multidomain C2 for joint and coalition audiences. Under the 505th, the 805th Combat Training Squadron (ShOC-N) is the lead venue for experimentation, testing, and development of technical solutions and tactics for JADC2. The 16th Air Force was created in October 2019 to provide CCMDs and the intelligence community with "combined [ISR], cyber,

---

[230] Hoehn, 2021a.

[231] Theresa Hitchens, "Exclusive JADC2 Strategy to Hit Milley's Desk in Days," *Breaking Defense*, February 8, 2021a.

[232] DAF official, interview with authors, March 24, 2021.

[233] A reviewer noted that as of April 2022, after our work was completed, the Chief Architect's Office was no longer connected to ABMS, and demonstrations had ceased.

[234] Allied and partner state participation is a stated goal for JADC2 experimentation, though participation has been limited to date.

[235] DAF official, interview with authors, July 12, 2021.

electronic warfare, and information operations."[236] The 16th Air Force is intended to support JADC2 by managing and defending a network to enable the fusion and sharing of data from across domains. Table B.1 summarizes the main players in JADC2—with a specific focus on the Air Force—and briefly describes their roles and responsibilities.

Table B.1. Main Stakeholders for JADC2

Organization	Role and Responsibility
JADC2 CFT	Primary lead for JADC2 efforts
JS J6	JADC2 CFT lead
Army	Project Convergence
Navy	Project Overmatch
DAF	
• ABMS CFT	• Strategic direction for DAF JADC2 activities; operational lead
• Rapid Capabilities Office	• Manages ABMS program of record; technical lead
• Chief Architect's Office	• Handled initial ABMS demonstrations
• Air Force Futures	• Lead for DAF's ABMS campaign design
• Air Combat Command	• Operational test and evaluation of the entire C2 portfolio, including the AOC
• 505th Combat Training Group	• Experimentation, tactics, and training for multidomain C2
• 805th Combat Training Squadron (ShOC-N)	• Experimentation, testing, and development of technical solutions and tactics
• 16th Air Force	• Managing and defending a network to enable the fusion and sharing of ISR and weather data from across domains
OSD (Research and Engineering)	Software architectures for JADC2
DoD CIO	Data and standards
OSD (Acquisition and Sustainment)	Acquisition oversight for JADC2
Kessel Run	C2 capabilities development for Air Force

Army

The Army's network needs under JADC2 will differ from those of the DAF. The Army requires a large-scale network capable of including many more sensors than other services; where an Air Force C2 network may have to tie together thousands of sensors, the Army may

---

[236] Tobias Naegele, "16th Air Force Is Fully Up and Running," *Air Force Magazine*, July 15, 2020.

have hundreds of thousands.[237] As the Army develops its long-range precision fire capabilities, it will rely on sensor data from joint systems to conduct strikes at strategic and operational distances. Similarly, it will rely on sensors in the air and space domains to defend against long-range strikes.[238] At a programmatic level, the Army desires to see greater commitment from the DAF to Project Convergence exercises. Army officials stressed that commitment needs to come from the most senior levels; without it, JADC2 development and exercises will not receive the joint resources—for example, F-35 flying hours—that are necessary to push the concept forward.[239]

The Joint Air Ground Integration Center (JAGIC) concept, which facilitates the integration of certain Army division staff with Air Force personnel involved in supporting ground operations,[240] may serve as an illustration of how the interface between the Air Force and Army may scale up to higher echelons in the future.[241] Existing training difficulties to support the JAGIC also indicate challenges for JADC2 training. JAGIC training has been hampered by the inability of Army simulations to take in ATOs from AOC systems and by the lack of access to AOC simulation capabilities for home-station training.[242] Addressing simulation interoperability and accessibility of simulation capabilities across the services will be key issues for JADC2 training.[243]

An example of a capability that the Army is developing illustrates some of the imperatives to increase simulation interoperability across domains. The Army is developing Air Launched Effects (ALEs), which are small, attritable UASs launched from aircraft that are fitted with sensors to capture and locate electronic signatures of hostile ground and airborne emitters. ALEs may provide ISR imagery and enable terminal guidance of munitions if they are employed to loiter over a target. Information gathered by ALEs has potential value to users across the structure envisioned by JADC2. Future aircraft avionics or airborne training add-on systems (e.g., pods) could contain the capability to simulate ALEs at the tactical edge. This would

---

[237] Greg Hadley, "Lack of JADC2 Coordination Across Services Is 'Recipe for Disaster,' Analyst Warns," *Air Force Magazine*, August 6, 2021.

[238] Andrew Feickert, *U.S. Army Long-Range Precision Fires: Background and Issues for Congress*, Congressional Research Service, R46721, March 16, 2021.

[239] Army officials, interview with authors, June 8, 2021.

[240] Specifically, personnel from the Tactical Air Control Party and Air Support Operations Center. Army Techniques Publication 3-91.1 and Air Force Tactics, Techniques, and Procedures 3-2.86, *The Joint Air Ground Integration Center*, U.S. Army, April 17, 2019.

[241] Army officials, interview with authors, June 8, 2021.

[242] Email communications with DAF officials.

[243] The battlefield coordination detachment (BCD)—an Army organization embedded within the AOC that helps integrate the C2 functions between the Air Force and Army—may serve as an organizational construct that could evolve to meet the operational and training needs of JADC2. For a discussion of the BCD in the context of multidomain operations, see Association of the United States Army, "Combined Joint Integration Detachment: The Next Evolution of the BCD," July 13, 2021.

exercise the entire sensor-to-shooter chain of data links and decisionmakers in a tactical framework.

Navy and Marine Corps

Naval Information Warfare Systems Command is primarily responsible for Project Overmatch. Naval Information Warfare Center (NIWC)-Pacific, NIWC-Atlantic's Seaworthy Artificial Intelligence Lab, and PEO C4I support Project Overmatch as well. Navy officials noted that whatever the Air Force develops for JADC2 (like ABMS) should allow for the Navy to use local instances of cloud-based resources, given the vulnerability of the Navy's C2 networks to denial and contestation.[244] The Marine Corps has no official office designated with JADC2 responsibilities, although there is an individual who serves as an informal JADC2 lead, participating in joint exercises and the JADC2 CFT.[245] To date, the Marine Corps has coordinated most closely with the Army and Navy and anticipates being closely aligned with the Navy's solutions for JADC2. A Marine Corps official expressed a desire to see increased Air Force participation in JADC2 events, for example, by providing airspace C2 and sorties for events. The same official noted that the Marine Corps and Navy would benefit from greater ATO integration with maritime and amphibious maneuvers, which could be enabled by ubiquitous connectivity with the Maritime Operations Center.[246]

---

[244] Navy officials, interview with authors, June 18, 2021.

[245] Marine Corps official, interview with authors, August 24, 2021.

[246] Marine Corps official, interview with authors, August 24, 2021.

Appendix C. How the Training Requirements Process and Task Lists Can Inform Training Objectives

Training Requirements Process

In addition to the parsing of training needs in Chapter 2, we reviewed the overall training process. Ideally, training needs and requirements for the use of simulation capabilities in training events could most easily be derived from authoritative task lists, such as the AFUTL or the UJTL.[247] The UJTL specifies military tasks that provide a capability for executing missions; it also provides a common language and a reference against which the individual services can define their own training tasks and draw links to how those tasks support broader joint tasks.

Although JADC2 is as of yet undefined in such task lists, we discuss how the joint requirements process may be used to identify requirements and develop capabilities for training for JADC2. We specifically note gaps in the process and how it might be improved.

Our crosswalk between the characteristics of JADC2 and a review of the UJTL reveal that tasks and related performance standards found in the UJTL would require greater granularity to help the services formulate and execute training for JADC2. For example, the UJTL task description for the operational C2 task "Communicate operational information" is "to send and receive operationally significant data from one echelon of command to another by any means." Standards for this task include the hours required for LNOs "to communicate new orders or information to allies and friendly elements of force."[248] The language for this task provides great latitude in how the services might train their C2 personnel. Greater specificity may be required to align service training with JADC2 requirements, which—to dwell on the example task above—will require new interactions across echelons and updated standards, for instance, moving away from a reliance on LNOs and toward faster, more-automated methods of communicating operational information.

Under JADC2, AOC personnel may require greater joint context and joint interactions in operational and tactical (tiers 3 and 4) C2 training.[249] However, the current training requirements process is not well designed to specify how JADC2 requirements might inform tiers 3 and 4 training for AOCs. When AOCs conduct CT, the tasks they train on generally come from their mission essential task lists (METLs). (See Figure C.1 for an illustration of how these lists are

---

[247] See CJCSM 3500.04F, *Universal Joint Task Manual*, Joint Chiefs of Staff, June 1, 2011, on service and joint task lists. Note that this discussion does not address requirements as part of the acquisition process; rather the discussion centers on training requirements that are accomplished in training events, such as virtual exercises.

[248] CJCSM 3500.04C, *Universal Joint Task List*, Joint Chiefs of Staff, July 1, 2002.

[249] Joint Staff officials, interview with authors, April 19, 2021.

used to inform training objectives.) These METLs are informed by the AFUTL and, one level up, by the UJTL.[250] As noted above, the granularity of these lists is not currently sufficient to specify how joint context might be injected in tiers 3 and 4 training via this training requirements process. Joint training requirements are rare at these tiers across the services, and there are organizational gaps in responsibilities to develop joint modeling and simulation training requirements specifically (i.e., it can be unclear who or which organization is responsible for setting specific training requirements).[251] Without more specificity in training requirements, and under the current training requirements process, it would be difficult to leverage these task lists *to identify where and how LVC might best be used* to support future JADC2 tasks.

One final issue with leveraging these lists for JADC2 training is that, in practice, AOCs pursue their organization's learning objectives when participating in CT exercises rather than aligning objectives explicitly with joint mission essential tasks (JMETs).[252] Thus, even assuming greater granularity in future task lists, there may have to be some forcing function—a formal doctrinal policy—to incentivize training planners to closely align their training events with joint tasks.[253]

Figure C.1 illustrates the relationship between joint task lists, the AFUTL, and the content of Air Force METLs, the elements of which are the primary drivers of units' training objectives. Although joint task lists inform the construction of the AFUTL,[254] units prioritize their core mission essential tasks (METs) in conducting training at tiers 3 and 4. As noted in Chapter 2, the content of the joint task lists does not provide sufficient guidance as to what the joint context of tasks at the lower tiers ought to be. Therefore, the existing process does not produce joint requirements at these lower tiers—that is, requirements including joint context in tiers 3 and 4 training events.

---

[250] Air Force Instruction 10-201, *Force Readiness Reporting*, Department of the Air Force, December 22, 2020.

[251] Timothy Marler, Matthew W. Lewis, Mark Toukan, Ryan Haberman, Ajay K. Kochhar, Bryce Downing, Graham Andrews, and Rick Eden, *Supporting Joint Warfighter Readiness: Opportunities and Incentives for Interservice and Intraservice Coordination with Training-Simulator Acquisition and Use*, RAND Corporation, RR-A159-1, 2021.

[252] DAF official, interview with authors, February 19, 2021.

[253] Joint Staff official, interview with authors, August 19, 2021.

[254] Air Force Instruction 10-201, 2020.

Figure C.1. Illustration of How Task Lists Inform Training Objectives

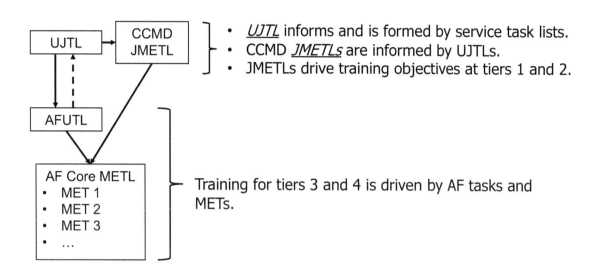

- *UJTL* informs and is formed by service task lists.
- CCMD *JMETLs* are informed by UJTLs.
- JMETLs drive training objectives at tiers 1 and 2.

Training for tiers 3 and 4 is driven by AF tasks and METs.

NOTE: JMETL = joint mission essential task list.

Appendix D. Air Operation Centers

Table D.1 lists the various AOCs we interviewed, including the type (geographic or global), the relevant command, and their location.

Table D.1. Air Force Air Operations Centers

Type	AOC	Command	Location
Geographic	601st	U.S. Northern Command	Tyndall AFB, Florida
Geographic	603rd	EUCOM and AFRICOM	Ramstein Air Base, Germany
Geographic	607th	INDOPACOM	Osan Air Base, South Korea
Global	608th	U.S. Strategic Command	Barksdale AFB, Louisiana
Geographic	609th	U.S. Central Command	Al Udeid Air Base, Qatar
Geographic	611th	U.S. Northern Command	Joint Base Elmendorf-Richardson, Alaska
Geographic	612th	U.S. Southern Command	Davis Mothan AFB, Arizona
Geographic	613th	INDOPACOM	Joint Base Pearl Harbor-Hickam, Hawaii
Global	614th	USSF	Vandenberg AFB, California
Global	616th[a]	CYBERCOM	Joint Base San Antonio-Lackland, Texas
Global	618th	U.S. Transportation Command	Scott AFB, Illinois
Global	623rd	AF Special Operations Command	Hurlburt Field, Florida

SOURCE: Adapted from Table 1.1 in Lingel et al., 2020.
[a] Sharon Singleton, "Air Force Information Warfare's New Warfighting Unit Activates," Air Combat Command, March 19, 2020.

Appendix E. ATO Stages, Basic Work Functions, and Approvals

Table E.1 lists the stages of the ATO process broken down by key components or substages. Also included are the basic work functions involved at each substage and the approvals needed.

Table E.1. Stages of the ATO Process

ATO Stages	Basic Work Functions	Approvals
Stage 1: Objectives, Effects, and Guidance		
Stage 1.1: JFC consultation with CCDRs	Information-gathering, information-sharing	
Stage 1.2: Air apportionment recommendation	Information-sharing	JFC
Stage 2: Target Development		
Stage 2.1: Update targeting database	Information-gathering, data management	
Stage 2.2: Target Effects Team prioritizes targets	Decisionmaking, information-gathering, data analysis	
Stage 2.3: Joint integrated prioritized target produced	Information-sharing	JFC
Stage 3: Weaponeering and Allocation		
Stage 3.1: Develop MAAP	Decisionmaking, information-gathering, data analysis	
Stage 3.2: Air allocation	Decisionmaking, information-sharing	
Stage 3.3: Allotment	Information-sharing, decisionmaking	JFACC
Stage 4: ATO Production and Dissemination		
Stage 4.1: ATO production	Writing	
Stage 4.2: ATO dissemination	Information-sharing, data management	
Stage 5: Planning and Force Execution		
Stage 5.1: Monitoring and redirection	Information-sharing, information-gathering, data analysis, decisionmaking	JFACC
Stage 5.2: AOC C2	Information-gathering, deconfliction, data analysis, information-sharing, decisionmaking	
Stage 5.3: Dynamic targeting	Information-sharing, deconfliction	
Stage 5.4: Priority revision	Information-sharing, deconfliction, decisionmaking	JFACC
Stage 6: Assessment		
Stage 6.1: Assessment protocol	Information-gathering, information-sharing	
Stage 6.2: Tactical assessment	Information-gathering, data analysis, information-sharing	
Stage 6.3: Operational assessment	Information-gathering, data analysis, information-sharing	

Appendix F. LVC State-of-the-Art Technologies

This appendix provides a brief overview of LVC technologies currently available in the commercial market that could augment training for JADC2 operations. Following the list of current capabilities is a list of developing capabilities, but the technology needs further development. However, these developing LVC capabilities should be monitored for future JADC2 training opportunities.

Given the perceived value and use of LVC generally, we review LVC-related technologies through the lens of relevance to JADC2. We align available tools and capabilities with JADC2 characteristics noted in Chapter 2 (and in Figure 2.1). Table F.1 lists LVC training tools available in the commercial market that the DAF and DoD could potentially use to enable and enhance JADC2 training. The table also includes potential training tools that are currently under development. Note that the most common LVC tools are listed to reflect the state of the art, but not all of them are applicable to JADC2.

As Table F.1 suggests, available tools align with JADC2 requirements in some way. However, many of these products are developed and managed by industry; DoD does not necessarily directly fund the development or maturation of these capabilities for DoD missions. Thus, it is in DoD's best interest to track relevant developments and augment funding when beneficial. Of course, Table F.1 also suggests that some current capabilities (for instance, three-dimensional [3D] spatial audio and orientational audio signals) are not necessarily relevant to JADC2 needs and thus need not be leveraged.

In subsequent discussion, we provide a brief description of each tool and then discuss which are most relevant to JADC2 and why. After reviewing technologies relevant to LVC in general, we then review systems specific to AOCs.

Table F.1. LVC Training Tools

LVC Training Tools		Potential JADC2 Implications			
		Decentralized C2, Dynamic Tasking	Distributed, Resilient C2, Devolution of Authorities	Faster C2 Processes	Inclusion of AI/ML Tools for Decision Support
Commercially Available	AR and VR head-mounted displays	X	X	X	X
	Heads-up displays (HUDs) and visors	X	X	X	X
	Domes, flat or curved	X	X	X	X
	Full-motion simulators	X	X	X	X
	Holographic images		X	X	X

LVC Training Tools		Potential JADC2 Implications			
		Decentralized C2, Dynamic Tasking	Distributed, Resilient C2, Devolution of Authorities	Faster C2 Processes	Inclusion of AI/ML Tools for Decision Support
In Development	3D spatial audio				
	Orientational audio signal				
	Haptics	X			
	Holonet (3D projections through lens)		X	X	X
	Brain-computer interfaces (haptic sensing of holographic images)	X			

SOURCES: Commercially available LVC technologies are derived from Timothy Marler, Susan G. Straus, Mark Toukan, Ajay K. Kochhar, Monica Rico, Christine Kistler LaCoste, Matt Strawn, and Brian Donnelly, *A New Framework and Logic Model for Appropriate Use of Live, Virtual, and Constructive Capabilities in Training*, RAND Corporation, 2023, Not available to the general public. The LVC technologies in development are derived from two sources: (1) David Cardinal, "Neural Holography Can Boost Real-Time VR, AR," *ExtremeTech*, August 26, 2020, and (2) Johns Hopkins University Applied Physics Laboratory, "Brain-Computer Interface Enables Johns Hopkins Study Participant to Touch and Feel Holographic Objects," *Newswise*, June 25, 2021.
NOTE: VR = virtual reality.

Current Capabilities

HMDs provide visual representation of a VR or AR world and enable users to interact with the environment based on how the head is oriented.[255] VR HMDs are immersive systems that can provide a complete simulated experience surrounding the user's head. The actual environment is not visible, blocking out the user's surroundings.[256] Alternatively, AR HMDs allow the user to view the real world and simulated objects in the real world. That is, AR HMDs enable the user to see the world around them augmented by constructive elements. HMDs in general are prevalent in the commercial market and have varying levels of fidelity and cost. The headsets can be tethered or untethered, the latter of which provides freedom of movement. Some limitations could include battery life (if untethered), limited bandwidth, limited depth perception, and limited resolution (or a combination of these).[257] HMDs can be integrated to support several

---

[255] Hua Li, Xin Zhang, Guangwei Shi, Hemeng Qu, Yanxiong Wu, and Jianping Zhang, "Review and Analysis of Avionic Helmet-Mounted Displays," *Optical Engineering*, Vol. 52, No. 11, 2013.

[256] Pietro Cispresso, Irene Alice Chicchi Giglioli, Mariano Alcañiz Raya, and Giuseppe Riva, "The Past, Present, and Future of Virtual and Augmented Reality Research: A Network and Cluster Analysis of the Literature," *Frontiers in Psychology*, Vol. 9, 2018; Will Greenwald, "Augmented Reality (AR) vs. Virtual Reality (VR): What's the Difference?" *PCMag*, March 31, 2021.

[257] Timothy Marler et al., 2023.

players in a single environment. They provide a wide field of view and low latency.[258] It is expected that headsets will become smaller, more mobile, and more powerful.[259]

HUDs or optical HUDs are another potential LVC training tool. The HUD is a new approach to presenting information to users. The user views a real scene and superimposed information simultaneously without large movements of the head or eye scans.[260] These tools provide a visual representation of an AR world (sometimes through such hardware as visors on helmets or ground-mounted like on a car window).[261] There are limitations with glare interfering with the training tool's processing of the real environment.[262] HUDs are available in the commercial market with varying levels of fidelity.

Large-screen, room-based displays (e.g., walkable domes, flat or curved panel systems) can accommodate small groups of participants that are presented with a shared, large-scale representation of scenes and objects within them. These systems vary in fidelity. Nonimmersive systems, which use desktops to reproduce images of the world, are the simplest and cheapest type of VR applications.[263] However, there are more-complex and extensive domes or curved screens, which provide a larger field of view.

Full-motion simulators (i.e., aircraft simulators) provide a semi-immersive environment. This integration of motion has now taken the form of enormous hydraulic lift systems that afford simulated motion in all directions. Simulators built on this technology have become the status quo in high-fidelity flight simulation.[264]

Holographic images are also available to provide VR. Holographic images use a laser light source to present a 3D image to the user.[265] Depending on the system, this image can move, so holographic images can be and have been used to create complete scenes. The holographic images can be presented from an external source, and wearables may not be necessary.

With **3D audio systems**, a user can detect whether a sound occurs in front or behind them, just as a person can detect whether sound happens in front of or behind them in reality. 3D audio

---

[258] Greenwald, 2021.

[259] Bernard Marr, "The 5 Biggest Virtual and Augmented Reality Trends in 2020 Everyone Should Know About," *Forbes*, January 24, 2020.

[260] Kikuo Asai, "The Role of Head-Up Display in Computer Assisted Instruction," in Kikuo Asai, ed., *Human-Computer Interaction, New Developments*, Intechopen, 2008; Richard L. Newman, *Operational Problems with Head-Up Displays During Instrument Flight*, Air Force Aerospace Medical Research Laboratory, AFAMRL-TR-80-116, 1980; Daniel J. Weintraub and Michael Ensing, *Human Factors Issues in Head-Up Display Design: The Book of HUD*, Crew Station Ergonomics Information Analysis Center, 1992.

[261] Weintraub and Ensing, 1992.

[262] Timothy Marler et al., 2023.

[263] Timothy Marler et al., 2023.

[264] Eric A. Vaden, *The Effect of Simulator Platform Motion on Pilot Training Transfer: A Meta-Analysis*, dissertation, Embry-Riddle Aeronautical University, Fall 2002.

[265] Cardinal, 2020.

is able to portray sound in a realistic fashion. The devices that support 3D audio depend on the placement of the head of the user, and because humans process sound differently due to the intricacies of the inner ear, there is variation in how people perceive sound.[266] Orientational audio cues provide the user with inputs based on sound.

Haptic gloves provide touch and pressure stimulus to an individual user.[267] Ongoing advances in haptic devices include the improvement of the sense of touch and manipulation of objects and feedback provided by wearable devices, as well as the incorporation of new computational techniques that dynamically improve the visual realism of a scene in real time.[268] Haptic suits or shirts are also able to provide input into systems and ensure that the surrounding system supports where a user's body is placed.

In summary, there is continual technology research to enhance the computing power, size, weight, performance, cost, and fidelity of the listed training tools. The DAF and DoD should stay abreast of these technology areas as well as some new potential training tools that are described in the state-of-the-art section below.

Developmental Capabilities

The previous section covered commercial training tools, but this section covers R&D efforts and advanced technology that may be available in the future. The developmental capabilities listed here are seen as novel. These systems are not merely advancements of previous LVC technologies; they incorporate new technologies (hardware and software). Perhaps most applicable to current LVC capabilities are such **ML AR systems** as holonet. Stanford University is developing this neural holography, which uses a specialized neural network trained with a camera-in-the-loop simulator to generate near-real-time images when the user looks through a lens.[269] These images can supplement AR and/or VR technology by enhancing the user's perception of the environment so that a user does not have to focus on an image presented on a two-dimensional screen. The system also enables 3D objects to appear from the user's perspective.[270]

Additionally, **brain-computer interfaces** are enabling users to "feel" virtual objects by integrating neural stimulation in a mixed-reality environment.[271] Users are reliant on their sensory organs to perceive the world around them; brain-computer interfaces are a pathway to transform the user's perception of their environment. The Defense Advanced Research Projects

---

[266] Timothy Marler et al., 2023.

[267] Timothy Marler et al., 2023.

[268] Timothy Marler et al., 2023.

[269] Cardinal, 2020.

[270] Cardinal, 2020.

[271] Johns Hopkins University Applied Physics Laboratory, 2021.

Agency is funding a research project called Neurally Enhanced Operations (NEO), wherein users can actually touch and feel holographic images presented through an AR HMD (Hololens).[272]

Implications for JADC2

As shown in Table F.1, there are multiple available and developmental technologies that may be relevant to LVC and to JADC2. Research continues to enhance the computing power, size, weight, performance, cost, and fidelity of these tools. Thus, the DAF and DoD should not only stay abreast of these technology areas but should support those that align with JADC2 requirements. When considering the implications discussed in Chapter 2, certain tools have notable potential impact.

Decentralized C2 and Dynamic Taskings

To enhance the evolution of decentralized C2, multiple personnel will have to carry out execution authorities to have an emergent effect, and they will need to be able to adapt to environments that change quickly, especially at AOCs. AR and VR HMDs, visors, and large-sized visual display systems (e.g., dome-based systems) can enable teams to connect and train to ensure that teams are able to respond simultaneously to achieve an effect in dynamic situations as would be required by an AOC. These tools allow users to encounter problems and practice decisionmaking that enables dynamic taskings simultaneously, as they would in a real-time global conflict.[273]

Distributed, Resilient C2 and Devolution of Authorities

C2 dynamic taskings should be able to integrate large groups of personnel in the C2 chain and support the flow of information among disparate and perhaps geographically distributed personnel at AOCs. For example, HMDs could enable multiple geographically disparate teams to be connected through the same global or theater-wide simulation to train on the full C2 chain, learn how C2 taskings are implemented, and ensure the execution of C2 is successful, even if decentralized.

Developmental technologies incorporating holographic methods can help users visualize information, objects, threats, and system interfaces. This could enable understanding of the environment and tools at their disposal; leaders could practice presenting new taskings and enabling faster C2 processes.

---

[272] Johns Hopkins University Applied Physics Laboratory, 2021.

[273] For example, USAF has worked with Immersive Wisdom and Entegra Systems to demonstrate distributed, real-time collaboration in a 3D immersive environment.

Faster C2 Processes

Users will need to practice C2 processes and ensure the flow of information from higher headquarters to lower echelons. These training tools enable multiple users to simulate a realistic environment and pass information, including taskings, feedback, and status updates, among the players.

Developing technologies, such as haptic sensors and brain-computer interfaces could eventually improve realism in training when executing C2 processes. An important potential attribute of brain-computer interfaces and haptic sensors is that users can physically and cognitively interact with the system that they will be using. This could be helpful for human-machine teaming. Although these capabilities are not yet mature enough for DoD applications, they are part of emerging commercial development efforts and experimental research efforts.

Inclusion of AI/ML Tools for Decision Support

To facilitate trust in the AI/ML tools that will help users understand the complex environment around them across multiple domains, practicing with AI/ML tools will be critical to the implementation of JADC2. The currently available tools enable users to practice understanding how AI/ML is presenting information that it has processed and to build trust in the tools.

By practicing with AI/ML tools, perhaps through mission planning with holograms and automated systems that optimize decisionmaking, the user can become more comfortable with AI/ML decision support and ensure it is employed correctly.

Orientational audio signals that use **3D spatial audio** technology do not have direct benefits for JADC2, unless close, real-time collaboration is occurring in a virtual setting with AOC participants distributed across different geographic locations, where spatial audio may enhance realism.

Abbreviations

13O	Multi-Domain Warfare Officer (Air Force Specialty Code)
3D	three-dimensional
A2AD	anti-access and area denial
ABMS	Advanced Battle Management System
ACC	Air Combat Command
ACC/A3C	ACC Command and Control, Intelligence, Surveillance, and Reconnaissance Operations Division (Airman Third Class)
ACE-IOS	Air and Space Cyber Constructive Environment—Information Operations Simulator
ADOC	all-domain operations center
AFAMS	Air Force Agency for Modeling and Simulation
AFB	Air Force Base
AFMSTT	Air Force Modeling and Simulation Training Toolkit
AFRICOM	U.S. Africa Command
AFSIM	Advanced Framework for Simulation, Integration and Modeling
AFUTL	Air Force Universal Task List
AI	artificial intelligence
AOC	air operations center
AOR	area of responsibility
AR	augmented reality
ASCCE	Air, Space, and Cyber Constructive Environment
ATARS	Airborne Tactical Augmented Reality System
ATO	air tasking order
BLCSE	Battle Lab Collaborative Simulation Environment
C2	command and control
C2IMERA	Command and Control Incident Management Emergency Response Application
C2SET	Command and Control Synthetic Environment for Training
C3	command, control, and communications
C4I	command, control, communications, computers, and intelligence
CCDR	combatant commander
CCMD	combatant command
CCW	Command and Control Wing
CFT	cross-functional team
CIO	chief information officer

CIP	Classification of Instructional Programs
CMR	combat mission ready
COMAFFOR	commander, Air Force forces
COP	common operating picture
CSpoC	Combined Space Operations Center
CSTE	Common Synthetic Training Environment
CT	continuation training
CTS	combat training squadron
CYBERCOM	U.S. Cyber Command
DAF	Department of the Air Force
DevSecOps	development, security, and operations
DIRLAUTH	direct liaison authorized
DoD	U.S. Department of Defense
ECWG	Exercise Coordination Working Group
EUCOM	U.S. European Command
EW	electronic warfare
FTU	formal training unit
HAF	Headquarters Air Force
HMD	head-mounted display
ILO	in lieu of
INDOPACOM	U.S. Indo-Pacific Command
IQT	initial qualification training
ISR	intelligence, surveillance, and reconnaissance
ISRW	Intelligence, Surveillance, and Reconnaissance Wing
IT	information technology
JADC2	Joint All Domain Command and Control
JADO	joint all-domain operations
JFACC	Joint Force Air Component Commander
JFC	joint force commander
JLCCTC	Joint Land Component Constructive Training Capability
JLVC	Joint Live Virtual Constructive
JMET	joint mission essential task
JS	Joint Staff
JSE	Joint Simulation Environment
JTSE	Joint Training Synthetic Environment
KRADOS	Kessel Run All Domain Operations Suite
LNO	liaison officer
LVC	live, virtual, and constructive (training capabilities)
MAAP	master air attack plan

MAJCOM	major command
MDOC	multidomain operations center
MET	mission essential task
METL	mission essential task list
MILS	Multiple Independent Levels of Security
ML	machine learning
MQT	mission qualification training
NAF	Numbered Air Force
NATO	North Atlantic Treaty Organization
OJT	on-the-job training
OPCON	operational control
OPR	office of primary responsibility
OPS	operations
OSD	Office of the Secretary of Defense
OTI	Operational Training Infrastructure
OTTI	Operational Test and Training Infrastructure
PAF	Project Air Force
PASC	Pacific Air Simulation Center
PEO	program executive officer
PMTEC	Pacific Multi-Domain Test and Experimentation Capability
R&D	research and development
ShOC-N	Shadow Operations Center-Nellis
SME	subject-matter expert
SPACECOM	U.S. Space Command
TACON	tactical control
TBMCS	Theater Battle Management Core System
TCTS	Tactical Combat Training System
TRS	training squadron
TTP	tactics, techniques, and procedures
UAS	unmanned aerial system
UJTL	Universal Joint Task List
USAF	U.S. Air Force
USSF	U.S. Space Force
VR	virtual reality

References

Air Combat Command, "Cyber Command and Control Mission System (C3MS)," webpage, January 24, 2020a. As of October 25, 2022: https://www.acc.af.mil/About-Us/Fact-Sheets/Display/Article/2241395/cyber-command-and-control-mission-system-c3ms/

Air Combat Command, *Rebuilding the Forge Concept of Operations*, Department of the Air Force, June 2, 2020b.

Air Force Doctrine Note 1-20, *USAF Role in Joint All-Domain Operations*, Department of the Air Force, March 5, 2020.

Air Force Doctrine Publication 1, *The Air Force*, Department of the Air Force, March 10, 2021.

Air Force Doctrine Publication 3-0, Operations and Planning, Department of the Air Force, November 4, 2016.

Air Force Doctrine Publication 3-30, Command and Control, Department of the Air Force, January 7, 2020.

Air Force Doctrine Publication 3-99, *Department of the Air Force Role in Joint All-Domain Operations (JADO)*, Department of the Air Force, October 8, 2020.

Air Force Instruction 10-201, *Force Readiness Reporting*, Department of the Air Force, December 22, 2020.

Air Force Instruction 10-204, *Air Force Service Exercise Program and Support to Joint and National Exercise Program*, Department of the Air Force, April 12, 2019.

Air Force Instruction 16-1005, *Modeling and Simulation Management*, Department of the Air Force, June 23, 2016.

Air Force Instruction 16-1007, *Management of Air Force Operational Training Systems*, Department of the Air Force, October 1, 2019.

Air Force Instruction 99-103, *Capabilities-Based Test and Evaluation*, Department of the Air Force, November 18, 2019.

Air Force Lessons Learned, *Doolittle Series 18: Multi-Domain Operations*, Air University Press, LeMay Papers, Vol. 3, 2019.

Air Force Space Command, *Air Force Space Command Live Virtual Constructive—Operations Training Review Report*, October 7, 2016.

"Air Force to Phase Out 13O Career Field, Strengthen All Airmen Joint Capabilities," U.S. Air Force, February 17, 2022.

Albon, Courtney, "Space Force Crafting Requirements for National Space and Test Training Range," *Inside Defense*, January 21, 2021a.

Albon, Courtney, "AFRL, Space Force Set Priorities for New Testing Enterprise," *Inside Defense*, February 3, 2021b.

"Alion Awarded $73 Million Task Order to Provide Joint Training Synthetic Environment Research and Development," PR Newswire, October 13, 2020.

Army Techniques Publication 3-91.1 and Air Force Tactics, Techniques, and Procedures 3-2.86, *The Joint Air Ground Integration Center*, U.S. Army, April 17, 2019.

Asai, Kikuo, "The Role of Head-Up Display in Computer Assisted Instruction," in Kikuo Asai, ed., *Human-Computer Interaction, New Developments*, Intechopen, 2008.

Association of the United States Army, "Combined Joint Integration Detachment: The Next Evolution of the BCD," July 13, 2021.

Bach, Deborah, "U.S. Army to Use HoloLens Technology in High-Tech Headsets for Soldiers," Microsoft, June 8, 2021.

Barrett, Barbara, and David L. Goldfein, *United States Posture Statement Fiscal Year 2021*, U.S. Air Force, 2020.

Builder, Carl H., *The Masks of War: American Military Styles in Strategy and Analysis*, Johns Hopkins University Press, 1989.

Cardinal, David, "Neural Holography Can Boost Real-Time VR, AR," *ExtremeTech*, August 26, 2020.

Carnegie Mellon University Software Engineering Institute, "DevSecOps," webpage, undated. As of September 20, 2021:
https://www.sei.cmu.edu/our-work/devsecops

Carpenter, Trent R., "Command and Control of Joint Air Operations Through Mission Command," *Air & Space Power Journal*, Summer 2016.

Chairman of the Joint Chiefs of Staff Instruction 1800.01F, *Officer Professional Military Education Policy*, Joint Chiefs of Staff, May 15, 2020.

Chairman of the Joint Chiefs of Staff Manual 3500.04C, *Universal Joint Task List*, Joint Chiefs of Staff, July 1, 2002.

Chairman of the Joint Chiefs of Staff Manual 3500.04F, *Universal Joint Task Manual*, Joint Chiefs of Staff, June 1, 2011.

Cispresso, Pietro, Irene Alice Chicchi Giglioli, Mariano Alcañiz Raya, and Giuseppe Riva, "The Past, Present, and Future of Virtual and Augmented Reality Research: A Network and Cluster Analysis of the Literature," *Frontiers in Psychology*, Vol. 9, 2018.

CJCSM—*See* Chairman of the Joint Chiefs of Staff Manual.

Cohen, Rachel S., "Moving MDC2 from Research to Reality," *Air Force Magazine*, April 15, 2019.

Collins Aerospace, "P6 Combat Training System (CTS)," webpage, undated. As of September 22, 2021:
https://www.collinsaerospace.com/what-we-do/Military-And-Defense/Simulation-And-Training/Test-And-Training-Instrumentation/P6-Combat-Training-System

Cook, Russell, *The Next Step: A Study on Resilience in Command and Control*, U.S. Air Force, June 1, 2015.

Crossan, Mary M., and Marina Apaydin, "A Multi-Dimensional Framework of Organizational Innovation: A Systematic Review of the Literature," *Journal of Management Studies*, Vol. 47, No. 6, 2010.

Datzman, Alicia, "Joint All-Domain Command and Control Operational Success Requires Investment in Multi-Domain Test and Training," *Modern Integrated Warfare*, November 25, 2019.

Defense Acquisition Management Information Retrieval, *2016 Major Automated Information System Annual Report, Air and Space Operations Center-Weapon System Increment 10.2*, March 2016.

Defense Modeling and Simulation Enterprise, "M&S Glossary," U.S. Department of Defense, March 19, 2014.

DeLong, Rance J., "MILS: An Architecture for Security, Safety, and Real Time," Tech Briefs, November 1, 2006.

Department of Defense Chief Information Officer, "DoD Enterprise DevSecOps Reference Design 1.0 Public Release," September 12, 2019.

Department of Defense Instruction 5000.02, *Operation of the Adaptive Acquisition Framework*, U.S. Department of Defense, January 23, 2020.

Department of Defense Instruction 5000.87, *Operation of the Software Acquisition Pathway*, U.S. Department of Defense, October 2, 2020.

Department of the Air Force, 505th Command and Control Wing, "Air Component Training Courses and Exercises," undated.

Department of the Air Force, *Small Unmanned Aircraft Systems (SUAS) Flight Plan 2016-2036: Bridging the Gap Between Tactical and Strategic*, April 30, 2016.

Department of the Air Force, *Air Force Operational Training Infrastructure 2035 Flight Plan*, September 5, 2017, Not available to the general public.

Department of the Air Force, "Presidential Budget," February 2018.

Department of the Air Force, "505 TTG TASKING ORDER 20-03 (505 TRS MDC2/Training Model CONOP)," January 29, 2020a.

Department of the Air Force, "505th Training Squadron Immersion Brief," June 26, 2020b.

Department of the Air Force, *Operational Test and Training Infrastructure (OTTI) 2035 Flight Plan Supplement for Command and Control*, forthcoming.

Department of the Air Force Manual 13-1AOC, Volume 1, *Ground Environment Training Air Operations Center (AOC)*, Department of the Air Force, July 29, 2019.

Deptula, David, and Douglas A. Birkey, "Potential Defense Budget Cuts Demand a New Calculus," *Defense News*, July 31, 2020.

Dideriksen, Amy, Christopher Reuter, Thomas Patry, Thomas Schnell, Jaclyn Hoke, and Jocelyn Faubert, "Define Expert: Characterizing Proficiency for Physiological Measures of Cognitive Workload," *Proceedings of the Interservice/Industry Training, Simulation, and Education Conference*, December 2018.

DoD—*See* U.S. Department of Defense.

DoD CIO—*See* Department of Defense Chief Information Officer.

DoD Instruction—*See* Department of Defense Instruction.

Dvorak, John, Roy Scrudder, Kevin Gupton, and Kevin Hellman, "Enabling Joint Synthetic Training Interoperability Through Joint Federated Common Data Services," *Cybersecurity & Information Systems Information Analysis Center Journal*, Vol. 7, No. 3, 2020.

Everstine, Brian W., "AFCENT Can Now Generate Air Tasking Orders in the Cloud," *Air Force Magazine*, May 14, 2021.

Feickert, Andrew, *U.S. Army Long-Range Precision Fires: Background and Issues for Congress*, Congressional Research Service, R46721, March 16, 2021.

Feickert, Andrew, *The Army's Project Convergence*, Congressional Research Service, IF11654, June 2, 2022.

Gallei, Francisco, "Multi-Domain Warfare Officer, the I3O," *Air Land Sea Bulletin*, No. 2020-1, Winter 2020.

Greenwald, Will, "Augmented Reality (AR) vs. Virtual Reality (VR): What's the Difference?" *PCMag*, March 31, 2021.

Hadley, Greg, "Lack of JADC2 Coordination Across Services Is 'Recipe for Disaster,' Analyst Warns," *Air Force Magazine*, August 6, 2021.

Harrison, Todd, "Battle Networks and the Future Force," Center for Strategic and International Studies, August 5, 2021.

Hawley, John K., "PATRIOT WARS: Automation and the Patriot Air and Missile Defense System," Center for a New American Security, January 2017.

Hitchens, Theresa, "Esper Orders SDA to Link C2 Networks for All-Domain Ops," *Breaking Defense*, May 6, 2020a.

Hitchens, Theresa, "MDA: All-Domain C2 Key to Countering Hypersonic Missiles," *Breaking Defense*, May 14, 2020b.

Hitchens, Theresa, "From 'Mad Hatter' to 'Torque': Kessel Run Makes Software for F-22, CV-22," *Breaking Defense*, July 21, 2020c.

Hitchens, Theresa, "Exclusive JADC2 Strategy to Hit Milley's Desk in Days," *Breaking Defense*, February 8, 2021a.

Hitchens, Theresa, "OSD, Joint Staff Double Down on DoD-Wide Data Standards," *Breaking Defense*, February 10, 2021b.

Hitchens, Theresa, "DARPA Builds AI to Avoid Army, AF Fratricide," *Breaking Defense*, February 17, 2021c.

Hitchens, Theresa, "ABMS Grows Up: Air Force Shifts Focus to Delivering Kit," *Breaking Defense*, May 24, 2021d.

Hitchens, Theresa, "Combatant Commands Worry About Service JADC2 Stovepipes," *Breaking Defense*, August 31, 2021e.

Hoehn, John R., *Joint All-Domain Command and Control (JADC2)*, Congressional Research Service, IF11493, version 15, July 1, 2021a.

Hoehn, John R., *Joint All-Domain Command and Control: Background and Issues for Congress*, Congressional Research Service, R46725, version 8, August 12, 2021b.

Horowitz, Michael C., "When Speed Kills: Lethal Autonomous Weapon Systems, Deterrence and Stability," *Journal of Strategic Studies*, Vol. 42, No. 6, 2019.

Hostage, Gilmary M. III, and Larry R. Broadwell, Jr., "Resilient Command and Control: The Need for Distributed Control," *Joint Force Quarterly*, Vol. 74, July 2014.

Jaime, Rick, and Steve Trnka, "AFMC ACC OTTI TASR Briefs—ACC Operational Test & Training Infrastructure (OTTI) Acquisition Approach," Air Force Materiel Command Air Combat Command, January 29, 2020.

Johns Hopkins University Applied Physics Laboratory, "Brain-Computer Interface Enables Johns Hopkins Study Participant to Touch and Feel Holographic Objects," Newswise, June 25, 2021.

Joint Publication 3-30, *Joint Air Operations, Joint Chiefs of Staff*, July 25, 2019.

Justice, Joseph H. III, "Airpower Command and Control: Evolution of the Air and Space Operations Center as a Weapon System," U.S. Army, March 19, 2004.

Kania, Elsa B., "Battlefield Singularity: Artificial Intelligence, Military Revolution, and China's Future Military Power," Center for a New American Security, November 2017.

Katz, Bruce, and Peter Ising, "Kessel Run Deploys KRADOS to Air Operations Center," Kessel Run, January 12, 2021.

King, William R., and Jun He, "A Meta-Analysis of the Technology Acceptance Model, *Information & Management*, Vol. 43, No. 6, 2006.

Landis, Ronald S., Lawrence Fogli, and Edie Goldberg, "Future-Oriented Job Analysis: A Description of the Process and Its Organizational Implications," *International Journal of Selection and Assessment*, Vol. 6, No. 3, 1998.

Leidos, "Command and Control Incident Management Emergency Response Application (C2IMERA)," fact sheet, undated.

LeMay Center for Doctrine Development and Education, *Annex 3-1 Department of the Air Force Role in Joint All-Domain Operations (JADO)*, June 1, 2020.

Li, Hua, Xin Zhang, Guangwei Shi, Hemeng Qu, Yanxiong Wu, and Jianping Zhang, "Review and Analysis of Avionic Helmet-Mounted Displays," *Optical Engineering*, Vol. 52, No. 11, 2013.

Lingel, Sherrill, Jeff Hagen, Eric Hastings, Mary Lee, Matthew Sargent, Matthew Walsh, Li Ang Zhang, and David Blancett, *Joint All-Domain Command and Control for Modern Warfare: An Analytic Framework for Identifying and Developing Artificial Intelligence Applications*, RAND Corporation, RR-4408/1-AF, 2020. As of October 25, 2022: https://www.rand.org/pubs/research_reports/RR4408z1.html

"Lockheed Martin Tasked to Integrate Battle Management Capabilities for USAF's KRADOS," Military & Aerospace Electronics, June 3, 2021.

Mahshie, Abraham, "VanHerck: SPACECOM 'Critical' to Latest High-Tech Exercise, but Hurdles Remain, *Air & Space Forces Magazine*, July 28, 2021.

Marler, Timothy, Matthew W. Lewis, Mark Toukan, Ryan Haberman, Ajay K. Kochhar, Bryce Downing, Graham Andrews, and Rick Eden, *Supporting Joint Warfighter Readiness: Opportunities and Incentives for Interservice and Intraservice Coordination with Training-Simulator Acquisition and Use*, RAND Corporation, RR-A159-1, 2021. As of October 25, 2022:
https://www.rand.org/pubs/research_reports/RRA159-1.html

Marler, Timothy, Susan G. Straus, Mark Toukan, Ajay K. Kochhar, Monica Rico, Christine Kistler LaCoste, Matt Strawn, and Brian Donnelly, *A New Framework and Logic Model for Appropriate Use of Live, Virtual, and Constructive Capabilities in Training*, RAND Corporation, 2023, Not available to the general public.

Marr, Bernard, "The 5 Biggest Virtual and Augmented Reality Trends in 2020 Everyone Should Know About," *Forbes*, January 24, 2020.

McCardle, Jennifer, "Victory over and Across Domains," Center for Strategic and Budgetary Assessments, January 25, 2019.

McFarland, Kevin, "Digital Engineering Shift and Simulation Vision: Common Synthetic Environment," NTSA Simulation Training and Community Forum, August 11, 2021.

Menke, Timothy, "Joint Simulation Environment for United States Air Force Test Support," *NATO Science and Technology Organization Meeting Proceedings*, STO-MP-MSG-171-17, October 18, 2019.

Mills, Patrick, James A. Leftwich, John G. Drew, Daniel P. Felten, Josh Girardini, John P. Godges, Michael J. Lostumbo, Anu Narayanan, Kristin Van Abel, Jonathan William Welburn, and Anna Jean Wirth, *Building Agile Combat Support Competencies to Enable Evolving Adaptive Basing Concepts*, RAND Corporation, RR-4200-AF, 2020. As of October 25, 2022:
https://www.rand.org/pubs/research_reports/RR4200.html

Morell, Stefan, "Optimizing Joint All-Domain C2 in the Indo-Pacific," *Air and Space Power Journal*, Summer 2021.

Moschellam, Joe, "AFMC ACC OTTI TASR Briefs—ACC Operational Test & Training Infrastructure (OTTI)," Air Force Materiel Command Air Combat Command, January 30, 2020.

Mulgund, Sandeep, "Evolving the Command and Control of Airpower," *Wild Blue Yonder Online Journal*, April 21, 2021.

Naegele, Tobias, "16th Air Force Is Fully Up and Running," *Air Force Magazine*, July 15, 2020.

National Institute of Standards and Technology Computer Security Resource Center, "Glossary," undated. As of January 4, 2023:
https://csrc.nist.gov/glossary

Newman, Richard L., *Operational Problems with Head-Up Displays During Instrument Flight*, Air Force Aerospace Medical Research Laboratory, AFAMRL-TR-80-116, 1980.

O*NET Online, "Command and Control Center Officers," webpage, undated. As of October 25, 2022:
https://www.onetonline.org/link/custom/55-1015.00

Office of the Under Secretary of Defense for Personnel and Readiness, *Joint Operational Training Infrastructure Strategy*, March 2020.

Pomerleau, Mark, "US Cyber Command Advances on Platform to Consolidate Its Myriad Tools and Data," C4ISRNET, November 2, 2020.

Priebe, Miranda, Douglas C. Ligor, Bruce McClintock, Michael Spirtas, Karen Schwindt, Caitlin Lee, Ashley L. Rhoades, Derek Eaton, Quentin E. Hodgson, and Bryan Rooney, *Multiple Dilemmas: Challenges and Options for All-Domain Command and Control*, RAND Corporation, RR-A381-1, 2020. As of September 13, 2021:
https://www.rand.org/pubs/research_reports/RRA381-1.html

Roaten, Meredith, "Air Force Looking to Boost Connectivity for Simulators," *National Defense Magazine*, July 22, 2021.

Ryan, Sherry D., David A. Harrison, and Lawrence L. Schkade, "Information-Technology Investment Decisions: When Do Costs and Benefits in the Social Subsystem Matter?" *Journal of Management Information Systems*, Vol. 19, No. 2, 2002.

Schepers, Jeroen, and Martin Wetzels, "A Meta-Analysis of the Technology Acceptance Model: Investigating Subjective Norm and Moderation Effects," *Information & Management*, Vol. 44, No. 1, 2007.

Sherman, Jason, "DOD Eyes $2.7 Billion Proposal to Wrap Half the Planet in Multidomain Test Range," *Inside Defense*, April 8, 2020.

Singleton, Sharon, "Air Force Information Warfare's New Warfighting Unit Activates," Air Combat Command, March 19, 2020.

Smith, Jeremy S., "Joint Simulation Environment," Naval Air Systems Command, NAVAIR public release 2018-356, 2018.

Space Development Agency, "Battle Management Command, Control, and Communication (BMC3)," webpage, undated. As of October 25, 2022:
https://www.sda.mil/battle-management/

Stout, William M. S., Vincent Urias, Brian P. Van Leeuwen, and Han Wei Lin, "Dynamic Cybersecurity Training Environments for an Evolving Cyber Workforce," Sandia National Laboratories, SAND2017-2452C, March 1, 2017.

Stouten, Jeroen, Denise M. Rousseau, and David de Cremer, "Successful Organizational Change: Integrating the Management Practice and Scholarly Literatures," *Academy of Management Annals*, Vol. 12, No. 2, 2018.

Tucker, Patrick, "AI Gives 'Days of Advanced' Warning in Recent NORTHCOM Networked Warfare Experiment," *Defense One*, July 29, 2021.

Urias, Vincent E., Brian Van Leeuwen, William M. S. Stout, and Han W. Lin, "Dynamic Cybersecurity Training Environments for an Evolving Cyber Workforce," *2017 IEEE International Symposium on Technology for Homeland Security Proceedings*, 2017.

U.S. Air Force, *Air Force Future Operating Concept: A View of the Air Force in 2035*, Department of the Air Force, September 2015.

U.S. Air Force Personnel Center, *Air Force Officer Classification Directory (AFOCD): The Official Guide to the Air Force Officer Classification Codes*, October 31, 2021.

U.S. Cyber Command, "US and Australia Sign First-Ever Cyber Agreement to Develop Virtual Training Range," December 4, 2020.

U.S. Department of Defense, *Summary of 2018 National Defense Strategy of the United States of America: Sharpening the American Military's Competitive Edge*, 2018.

U.S. Department of Defense, *DoD Enterprise DevSecOps Reference Design*, Version 1.0, August 12, 2019.

U.S. Department of Defense, *Command, Control, and Communications (C3) Modernization Strategy*, September 2020a.

U.S. Department of Defense, *Electromagnetic Spectrum Superiority Strategy*, October 2020b.

U.S. Department of Defense, *DoD Enterprise DevSecOps Reference Design: CNCF Kubernetes*, Version 2.0, March 2021.

Vaden, Eric A., *The Effect of Simulator Platform Motion on Pilot Training Transfer: A Meta-Analysis*, dissertation, Embry-Riddle Aeronautical University, Fall 2002.

Volpe, Carrie, "609th AOC Optimizes ATO Production, First to Use KRADOS Operationally," U.S. Air Force, May 7, 2021.

Weintraub, Daniel J., and Michael Ensing, *Human Factors Issues in Head-Up Display Design: The Book of HUD*, Crew Station Ergonomics Information Analysis Center, 1992.

Wilson, Heather, and David L. Goldfein, *USAF Posture Statement Fiscal Year 2020*, U.S. Air Force, 2019.

Winkler, John D., Timothy Marler, Marek N. Posard, Raphael S. Cohen, and Meagan L. Smith, *Reflections on the Future of Warfare and Implications for Personnel Policies of the U.S. Department of Defense*, RAND Corporation, PE-324-OSD, 2019. As of October 25, 2022: https://www.rand.org/pubs/perspectives/PE324.html

Yates, Nick, "OTTI Update: Synthetic Test and Training Capability," presentation, NTSA Simulation Training and Community Forum, August 11, 2021.

Ingram Content Group UK Ltd.
Milton Keynes UK
UKHW050832020523
421094UK00007B/15